Henpecked

Henpecked

Aman Karan

authorHOUSE®

AuthorHouse™
1663 Liberty Drive
Bloomington, IN 47403
www.authorhouse.com
Phone: 1-800-839-8640

First published by AuthorHouse   11/04/2011

ISBN: 978-1-4567-8611-3 (sc)
ISBN: 978-1-4567-8678-6 (ebk)

Printed in the United States of America

Any people depicted in stock imagery provided by Thinkstock are models, and such images are being used for illustrative purposes only.
Certain stock imagery © Thinkstock.

This book is printed on acid-free paper.

Because of the dynamic nature of the Internet, any web addresses or links contained in this book may have changed since publication and may no longer be valid. The views expressed in this work are solely those of the author and do not necessarily reflect the views of the publisher, and the publisher hereby disclaims any responsibility for them.

Aman Karan also writes blogs that focus mainly on issues pertaining to his country, India. Currently, he is associated with news-portal www.MeriNews.com, writing under the penname Jay Hind. His homepage is www.merinews.com/cj/pankaj_kumar.

To date, the author has blogged thirteen articles through the MeriNews platform:

1. Let the UN utilise stashed black money for ailing economies
2. Disputed land in Ayodhya should be used for development purpose.
3. Does India require parliamentarians and politicians?
4. Indian legislators need to cut down on wasteful living
5. Full Democracy: Call back a failed government . . .
6. Telecom firms cheating customers with dubious alerts
7. Government needs to wake up against ignorance to researchers
8. Inadequate stipend-packages deter talent
9. Research, as career option
10. Dhoni must focus on his captaincy
11. Attacks on Indians in Australia: Time to introspect
12. Central Police: the need to fight terrorism
13. Commonwealth Games: A matter of embarrassment for India (http://humour.merinews.com/clogarticle.jsp?artic leID=15831985&category=Sports&catID=5)

To

all members of my sweet family.

Preface

We, in our family, lack one sister. Nevertheless, we are surrounded by nine sister-cousins in our entire family. Before I started scribbling this piece of family drama in 2003, I was largely moved by the first two seasons of the American family television comedy *Boy Meets World*, which represented a sweet family almost like ours. Though little Morgan Matthews had the fewest words to utter in those episodes, her character made me yearn for a young sister, whom I could care for and show affection to the same way little Matthews was cared for and loved.

My hankering for a sweet young sister brought to life the character of Renee, whose disposition incorporates more or less the features of my cute and sweet little sister-cousins as I remember them in the late '90s. Renee is lovable, beautiful, and charming—a young girl who enjoys a warm relationship and fond friendship with her big brother Matt.

Although Renee is the protagonist character, and her upbringing is monitored and guided enthusiastically by her brother Matt, it is actually Matt who is the lead character of this family drama. And his primary goal is to nurture his marital relationship with Sophie. The story, in parallel, covers Matt and Sophie's marital relationship and slowly shifts focus to a serious battle caused by a pointless misunderstanding, which seriously threatens their relationship.

However, our heroic Renee has her role to play in later parts too, as she heals an injured Matt, rescues him from ruffians, and supports him in saving his marriage. Renee understands that she is totally committed to her relationship with her brother and is ready to renounce her world for a reunion of Matt and Sophie. But, as usual, we find that it's basic human understanding that solves the strife that people endure from day to day. Matt is possessed of inherent troubleshooting characteristics and expects Sophie to conform to his ways instead of fighting against them. As soon as one realizes, as Sophie's insight says, one's own responsibilities and commitment requisite for strengthening bonds, one can overcome any issue in life and in a family.

My writing and subjects are mainly influenced by matters I encounter all the time as I observe people's lives in this world. *Henpecked* is compiled basically from lifestyles of people, conventions of families, and events in people's life. A television program I watched during early 2000s was about a group of young girls who were participating in teen beauty pageant. This idea prompted me to create the Miss New York Teen event for one leading lady in my story, and I believe this inspired me to write about Renee in her teen years. And only this thought drove me to start composing this book.

Naughty behaviours add spice to life, so the story's lead characters behave mischievously. We want to live happily and share happy moments in a family. We want to be spirited and accomplished in our world, and for that we want to be supported, encouraged, and hailed by our own people first. We want our success and achievements to be shared by our family members and friends. We want to live our lives with cooperation, affection, and love—and, of course, with some money. I think this is what 'life' is called—loving to be loved!

Once we comprehend the mettle of the characters in our story and learn to respect the personas they represent, we may see those qualities in people we meet in real life. Or, we may want to emulate those qualities in our own lives.

Acknowledgements

I am obliged to my parents for my upbringing and all of their support during my college days when I struggled a lot and suffered with depression over many failures. My family members have always been there to cherish me and keep my spirits up and to see me successful. I thank all of my mentors, who have always wanted me to touch excellence in my pursuits, and, indeed, have encouraged me to pursue success over anything else. I feel grateful to the Indian Institute of Technology Kharagpur too where the milieu, life experiences, and tempo have stimulated me to keep starting fresh endeavours in order to be hailed or at least noticed. There is a line drawn in our lives that clearly separates the success meant for us and failures that we can leave behind.

ONE

The atmosphere is formal and festive as guests gather at the outdoor gala wedding reception at the Grove Bracket Restaurant at a posh hotel on Lexington Avenue in midtown Manhattan. Sixteen-year-old Renee Dion passionately observes the gaiety as it is her family's celebration: the groom is her brother, Matt Dion. Presently, Matt is standing on dais at far end of the venue with his new wife, Sophie Jones Dion, as they receive felicity, blessings, and lot of expensive gifts. Renee's parents, Mrs. and Mr. Dion, are busy greeting guests at their son's wedding celebration.

The orchestra plays soothing classical music that maintains a tranquil ambience. The spacious grove, the dappled sunlight, and the beautifully outfitted dining tables add to the formality of the scene, while majestically dressed guests are also in no mood to break the charm of the atmosphere. Renee is resplendent in a catchy Mori Lee's quinceanera floor-length organza ball gown of bright purple, which is sleeveless and has a strapless neckline and is embellished with soft flowers, appliqués, and crystals that altogether reveals Renee's hourglass bust and narrow hips. Her thick, dark, shiny hair is beautifully arranged, a glittering golden chain adorns her pinkish bust, and long carved ear pendants dangle and catch the light. Renee has already moved to every corner and greeted almost all the guests, impressing them with her warmth. She is particularly proud of her appearance, which she has been designing for the past couple of weeks. However, the response to her exorbitant preparations hasn't been pleasing to Renee; she is eager to find someone who will appreciate her enthralling appearance and demeanour. Guests seem lost in relishing the party as if they came to revel only. Indeed, Renee is in no mood to endure the dullness of such an extravagant event. It is causing her painful boredom and making her tired as well. Nevertheless, she keeps displaying enthusiasm in entertaining guests.

On her way once again around the room, Renee joins a gathering of old men, busy toasting among themselves. 'Are you getting bored?' she asks them.

One of the gentlemen turns to her. 'No my dear! We well enjoy this flamboyant, sumptuous treat! Renee, your brother Matt is quite the handsome man! And his wife, too, possesses eminent grace and pulchritude. God bless the couple! Thanks for inviting us!'

Renee observes Mr. Matt Dion and Mrs. Sophie Dion at far end of the venue. Of course, they are clad beautifully in wedding regalia and look terrific. Sophie's dress is sleeveless with a sweetheart neckline and detachable chapel train. The Vera Wang white tulle gown is embellished with ruching, embroidery with metallic and pearl accents, beautiful beaded flowers, and sequins. She wears a matching tulle headpiece along with jewellery of gems, pearls, rhinestones, and crystal beadings. Sophie is a complete and beautiful bride. Matt's apparel includes a Tommy Hilfiger slim-fit, single-breasted, smooth, black tuxedo jacket over flat-front pants, a Calvin Klein watch, and a pair of Hugo Boss Calmon Oxfords shoes.

After the exchange of some pleasant smiles with the old men, Renee immediately alters her mood; her face becomes sullen. Having been disregarded in the appreciation of her marvellous attire and elegance, and dying of boredom, she considers it better to desert the people who are causing her mood. She moves on and looks at the bar, which is decorated in grandiose style with expensive brands of alcoholic beverages. Though waiters are serving drinks regularly and on demand, few men have assembled there. Renee feels utterly fatigued in dealing with these tired people. And what has happened to her circle of friends? She usually has them wrapped around her little finger, and they are always ready for a party! Needless to say, the presence of their parents and the rules of etiquette have discouraged her peers from boisterous partying.

Renee glances all around. Her parents are involved with their circle of friends. The newlyweds are busy enjoying their fresh marital status and appreciating the inevitable advice they are receiving. Renee's buddies, though they showed an enthusiastic reaction to her glance, do not seem to be inclined to party at such a grand occasion, and they have turned to the offering of gourmet food instead. The older men of her dad's circle are someway lost in their revelling at the bar. Renee is determined to have some fun at her family's unique gala on this majestic evening.

She pauses and again looks at the dullness all around. No one seems motivated to join her in happy celebration. So, she moves to the bar. The bartender does not notice Renee's motivation, and only frowns. But Rene is determined. She browbeats him into noticing her. Finally, he displays his appreciation, and asks her for her order. She requests a glass of chilled Chateau Cheval Blanc—1990. As she receives it, one of the old men gazes at Renee, slightly stunned. But she smiles pleasantly at him and clicks her glass to his.

Renee immediately walks away so as not to be interrupted by others, especially those who are close to her. Feeling revitalized, she walks directly to the band. She feels a bizarre sort of mood come over her as she swallows the last of her bubbly wine, and she is in no mood to chase it away. Suddenly, the orchestra comes to the end of one of their boring classical pieces. Renee begins to sway to a rhythm in her own head. She grabs the drumsticks from the drummer, and begins to rap out the rhythm on his drums.

Thank God! Her actions seem to be generating some interest. Some of her friends gather around. Several of them begin to cheer. Her parents take care to cover their ears, and Matt finds himself having to maintain the his dignity by to encouraging his guests to enjoy Renee's antics. The orchestra members are forced to vacate the field as Renee's young friends seize their spaces and their instruments. The professionals hope that their instruments will remain undamaged throughout the performance. The young people have played this particular composition at school functions, and Renee has been careful to choose only those fellows whom she knows she can wheedle into having a little fun. Renee's band fills the venue with lively music. As the song comes to an end, an attendant slips a note to Renee: 'Those instruments are very expensive. I beg you take care! —Matt'

Renee sees a pleading Matt at far end of the venue, and she decides to spare her brother any pain on his special day. However, as the orchestra members return to their instruments, she reminds them they are not being paid to kill the festive atmosphere of such a rare family event. This is a moment for lively celebration. The orchestra strikes up a salsa, and Renee and her friends begin to dance. She reaches Pete Boucher—her tall and attractive classmate who is often referred to as her beau. But Renee is disturbed to see him dancing with the enchanting lass Miss Ashley Jones—Renee's new sister-in-law and Sophie's sister. She allows them to take only a few more steps before she intrudes, embracing Pete. As she puts her hands over his back, she drives Ashley aside. Ashley is somewhat astounded over Renee's move, but perceives it better to join others. Pete smiles, but it is obvious that he is grumpy and unhappy at being parted from the pretty Ashley. Renee wishes to punch Pete hard but considers it better to abide by some reservations. She leaves Pete after a while as he purposely proves a fool. His seeming disinterest in her makes her cross and lessens her hankering for him. She steps away from him and leaps directly at her daddy. But Mr. Dion is in no mood to cut short his fun because of his daughter, so he clings to Mrs. Dion. Hurriedly, all other people seem to follow Mr. Dion's actions. They choose partners and begin to dance. Renee hugs Matt, but Sophie breaks them up with a clever step and seizes her new husband in a firm clutch.

Regardless, Renee invites some of the young men to dance with her. They comply obligingly and do not dampen her motivations because they do not want to break the formality of the occasion.

TWO

At home, Renee intercepts Matt and Sophie before they retire to their room. Matt pleads with her to let them go inside as it's past midnight and everyone has gone home. 'My dear sister,' he says wisely and overly tenderly in an attempt to evade her attentions, 'I saw that you seemed weary throughout the function despite the fact that you had taken on the burden of keeping everyone amused there. Now, I find you totally fatigued, and I think it would rather be best for you to get some deep sleep for your health. And, you are going to school, too, tomorrow morning. Good night!' he finished, trying to hasten their parting.

'Smart man,' retorts Renee, impervious to his evading tactics, 'can't you just say you don't want to talk to me because it will just delay your special night? I understand your rush to accomplish your marital relationship. But you must know that I have worked very hard and spent a lot of money to help make this dreamy night extravagant for you. I made your room look quite large with only minimal decoration and new shades of colours. The new tapestries at the windows are remotely controlled, and the chocolate-brown burlap that covers the ceiling contrasts with the puffy chocolate-brown carpet. The light installation allows you to change the colours of the light in your room in ten ways. The bathroom is provided with a huge bathtub in the latest fashion, and there are more extraordinary fixtures for maintaining privacy in your marital life. It shouldn't be difficult for you to calculate the value of my services. So, how do you think I should be rewarded?' she finishes, slightly impudent.

Matt seems let down and tries to evade her. 'When your day comes,' he promises her, 'I will make your wedding celebration more extravagant than mine, I promise. Now let Sophie and I experience the results of your kind services . . . please!'

Renee speaks hurriedly and in a whisper to Matt so that Sophie might not hear: 'There is a new motorbike on the market. I hate your obsolete bike—it has lots of problems and doesn't even have a smooth ride. I hope you will consider purchasing a new one soon!'

Matt only nods his head in the affirmative, since he is in a hurry to get inside the room.

Inside the room, Matt plays with the light system, changing colours frequently, which amuses him. He wants to find the loveliest shade for the room. As he turns of the light to soft, raspberry pink, Sophie enters the room in a beautiful bridal chemise of ivory silk trimmed in lace with matching lace jacket. Matt is stunned and stops playing with the lights. He stops breathing as he observes Sophie's svelte body and comely figure. Sophie blushes and smiles, which draws him close to her.

Matt shares a deep kiss with Sophie. He embraces her tightly. Feeling her body close to his, he is deeply stirred, unable to feel anything else. Sophie responds to Matt's embrace, and runs her fingers through his hair as she breathes deeply to control herself.

Afterwards Matt is lost with Sophie . . .

THREE

Renee gets up and is ready to leave for school. She joins the family at breakfast. But she immediately begins to sulk because the breakfast is missing her favourite foods. She loves blueberry pancakes soaked with maple syrup, French toast laced with fruit and cream, cheesecake, bacon rolls, chicken wraps, fried steak, waffle fries, sausage patties, cookies, and hot chocolate. In contrast, she sees only available fruits, fruit juice, cornflakes with hot milk, boiled eggs, sausages, bubble and squeak, omelette and toast (without butter, cheese, ham, and jam), baked beans with tomato sauce, baked mushrooms, and sliced tomatoes. At least there was coffee to wash it all down with.

Renee spoke to her father, who was busily consuming his breakfast. 'Is this an omelette?' she asked. 'Where are your minced meat croquettes, bacon, scrapple, and oatmeal pudding? Where are the fried eggs and grilled tomatoes?'

'Those items are not available today,' said Mr. Dion between bites. 'But cook is preparing spaghetti with scrambled eggs and grilled kippers also, especially for you. I know you like them because you and your brother always fight over them!'

'Pshaw,' snorted Renee. 'I stopped eating tasteless, over-boiled spaghetti long ago!' In walked Sophie carrying a platter of spaghetti.

'Here you go,' said Sophie as she placed the platter on the table. 'Matt has demanded this for breakfast. And my new daddy has to avoid eating too much cholesterol-rich food. From now on, we will be relishing delicacies full of healthful nutrients!'

She seeks support from Renee over the meal menu by fondling Renee's hair. But today's breakfast does not stimulate Renee's palate. She gives up rather early. Sophie looks askance at Renee.

Renee turns her attention to her father, who is still enjoying his breakfast. 'Daddy, if you don't mind . . . I am participating in the city teen beauty pageant from my school, and I will have to spend much money on costumes, cosmetics, and other fashion accessories. Besides, my circle of friends, including Pete and Sheila—as you know they are my best friends—are expecting a celebration at the school canteen over my brother's wedding.' As she finishes her speech, she minces her words. 'I need some three hundred dollars today.'

Sophie, seeming surprised at Renee's request, interrupts with a didactic speech. 'What a prodigal daughter!' she shrieks. 'Extravagance is over now! You are going to take your lunch to school today. The junk foods you are used to have little nutritional value, something I think you know quite well, being as you are a senior student at school.'

Renee, at first, finds it useless to squabble with the new member of her family when her daddy is lost in the so-called 'delicacies' served by this new and enchanting home and family manger. Renee finds it better to go to her room and collect her schoolbag. But she fails to find the bag overflowing with paraphernalia that she had packed the day before.

'Mum!' she screams, running back into the dining room. 'Mum, where is my bag?'

Mrs. Dion is busy clearing the table. 'It's in your room, my baby!'

Renee, boggled, returns to her room. 'No,' she yells down the stairs, 'it's not here!'

Mrs. Dion continues her home chores downstairs. But she assuredly suggests to Renee, 'It's where you left it. Just look!'

Renee is frustrated. 'Where?'

Sophie comes into Renee's room to handle her sister-in-law's problem. 'Look, dear,' she says, affecting surprise, 'it's right here on your study table. And you couldn't see it?'

Renee is amazed when she looks on her table and finds only a small bag, which contains only books. She is flabbergasted and peevish. 'Are you joking? How can this small bag contain all the belongings I'm going to need for the showy event at my school? This small bag does even not belong to me!' She looks crossly at Sophie. 'This bag cannot carry my costumes, makeup, accessories, high heels, laptop, sound amplification system, and many other things. Where are my things?'

Sophie remains calm, obviously impervious to Renee's ranting. 'Actually,' she said, 'you go to school for study and not for fun. Today your brother asked me to help you in arranging your schoolbag. When I checked your school diary, I discovered which classes are scheduled for today, and I determined which books you would need. You are required to perform academically extraordinarily if you aim to go on to college for higher studies. The other events in your curriculum are marked 'optional'. And I told your brother and your mummy too that you would be better off concentrating on your studies for a better career. I hope you understand the value of these facts, and will no longer feel the need for wasteful items in your schoolbag.'

The entire conversation is irritating to Renee. She grabs up the small bag and leaves her room to get away from Sophie and to leave the house so she won't miss school bus. However, as she nears the front door, she encounters her mother. 'Mum,' she whines, 'why couldn't you take care of my schoolbag after I arranged it so carefully? What is the problem with you?'

Mrs. Dion speaks to her daughter calmly. 'I have always asked you to take care of your own tasks yourself. You should not depend on me or your brother Matt to take care of your tasks. You are in twelfth grade now. Don't depend on others so much. And you should show some sincerity in your studies also.'

'Damn it!' frets Renee. 'I didn't come here to be instructed by everyone. Where is Matt?'

'Do you still hope him to be at home?' gibed Mrs. Dion. 'Having had a very early breakfast, he expeditiously left for work.'

Renee seems stunned at this fact about Matt. Putting her hands at her sides in frustration, she squealed, 'Big Brother, I will see you this evening!'

FOUR

Renee is sitting in the extracurricular activities period, but she is not taking part in the activities. Most of her classmates are busy at the concert centre learning music and dance routines, and rehearsing plays. Some others are rehearsing their ramp walk on stage in the auditorium nearby. Renee had also planned to participate in a beauty contest at the city level, but all of that seems doubtful now.

Many boys have gathered in the auditorium to observe these beautiful and talented young girls as they rehearse. Renee has none of her paraphernalia because her new sister-in-law had snatched it all away from her earlier in the morning. She wanders around by herself, unable to enthral the boys. She comes out of the dressing room and takes a seat in the nearly empty audience. Her disposition is lackadaisical as she watches the participants' rehearsal. In the absence of schoolteachers and other authoritarians, the boys occasionally burst into wild clapping and hooting when they appreciate a particular performer's style.

Some of Renee's classmates find her sitting in the audience dressed in her school uniform rather than performing onstage in her fashionable outfits. It's a matter of surprise to them that the girl who has the highest stake is not participating in the rehearsals. Some troublemakers turn relentlessly against Renee. One of them pesters her. 'Look . . . Miss New York Teen is here in her school uniform. Look at her superb performance in her very special costume! Let's applaud her excellent gait!'

The boys begin to clap and yell. All of this negative attention irritates Renee unquestionably. As usual, she jumps from her seat and chases the boys. They run, but several of them stumble, affording Renee the opportunity to apply a few well-aimed karate kicks. Meanwhile, instructors enter in the auditorium to see the progress of the rehearsal.

One of the instructors is obviously surprised to see the rampage going on. 'What is happening here?' she shouts. 'Renee, what are you doing here? Why are you not rehearsing with your costumes? Have you practiced your entire performance?'

Renee answers sheepishly. 'Sorry . . . I forgot to pack my bag because of a celebration in my family last night. And my new sister-in-law mistakenly packed my bag this morning according only to my study programs without considering my participation in the beauty event. I beg your pardon!' She has no idea how to explain the problem she is facing. Rather she tries to just cover it up.

The instructor is annoyed. 'How could you be so careless? Particularly at this moment! Don't you know that you are the lead participant from our school, and we are relying utterly on you for our school's standings in the competition? All of our efforts on your behalf seem to be just a waste of time now. The principal wants to watch today's rehearsal to check the progress. What will I respond her?'

Renee stands quietly, unable to answer. The instructor, still clearly upset, calms down a bit. 'Go immediately to the dressing room', she instructs Renee, 'and ask for help from other participants . . . we can't see you back out now.'

Renee walks off to the dressing room, followed by the instructor. It's not easy for her to tackle the awkward circumstance. But her mates are there to help her, so she relaxes. At the request of the instructors, other participants share their costumes and makeup with Renee. Finally, despite the difficult start, Renee performs before the principal and wins appreciative applause.

FIVE

Though infuriated, Renee strolls in the garden at home, trying to achieve a relaxed mood as she lies in waiting. Mrs. Dion has returned from the clinic where she is a medical specialist. She is relaxed too in the evening, and is now watering the orchids. Mrs. Dion smiles when she finds her babe is cooling her heels by pacing back and forth. She had earlier asked Renee's help in the watering, but Renee hadn't shown any interest in abiding by her mum's request.

As they enjoy the peace of the garden, the property gate slides open upon a silent electronic signal. They hear the sound of a large vehicle in the driveway. It is Mr. Dion, who is a senior officer in a law enforcement department. But, at the moment, he is a useless old man to Renee. Today he returns rather earlier in the evening than he is used to, just to enjoy the extra caring from his daughter-in-law. He is not inclined a bit to deal with the problems of his daughter, especially as they could only provide him with unwanted jitters. He enters the garden and meets Renee midway in her pacing. He quickly kisses her with only a quick check of her innocent doe eyes. He pretends all is well to avoid a crisis from the minx.

'How do you do, my baby?' says Mr. Dion to his daughter. 'I am somewhat tired. Can we have the tea now? Sophie must be ready with tea, and I am ready for refreshment.' Mr. Dion studiously ignores the perturbed countenance of Renee and goes inside in haste.

For Renee, her dad has become a busy old man, today intent on taking care of his matters only. 'But where is my brother Matt?' she wonders. Why has he not returned home early to his loving new wife, who should be the most important thing to him now? He is very late. Matt usually returns home by seven o'clock. Renee checks the time on her wristwatch.

Then, to Renee's relief, she hears the gate open again. It rolls aside slowly. She looks outside and is pleased to see her brother's familiar blue Ford Taurus SE swiftly enter the parking plot.

Matt comes into the house to face Renee eye to eye. Perceiving Renee's mood, he deliberately yawns widely to hint at the fatigue his day has caused him. But he cannot elude Renee so easily. He rubs Renee's hair and gives her a mock sneer. 'How was your day in school?' he asks. 'How are your studies going? You should be sitting at the study table in your room instead of loitering here.'

This is a great deal of mischief from Matt, who then tries to move further inside the house hastily. But, just as he is about to enter the living room, he is intercepted with a hard punch of irritation on his back.

Renee is clearly frustrated. 'Smart man, is this the time to return home?'

Matt rubs his sore back vigorously. 'Mum!' he calls out in fury.

Renee, spewing out fury in a similar fashion, retorts, 'It wasn't so hard! Just mind your legs—I am going to strike them next!'

Matt considers it better to leave the turf and runs for the shelter behind Mrs. Dion, who has just arrived after hearing the commotion. Matt speaks craftily, 'Mum, tell Renee that she is not my wife! I should explain my late arrival only to my wife!'

Renee is enraged. 'You try to collude against me!' she shouts. 'I will shatter your new wings, Mr. Aircraft Engineer!'

Matt retorts by shamming. 'Boohoo! Your new sister-in-law is inside. Why are you fighting with me?'

In the meantime, Sophie joins them to call them for tea. She seems very glad to see Matt there. He immediately hugs her, and she says, 'O dear . . . you are back—but little late!' She kisses her husband, then says cheerfully, 'Come inside. Let's have tea!'

Matt keeps his arm around his wife and moves inside indicating to Mrs. Dion and Renee that they should follow. As they do, he turns and sticks out his tongue at Renee mischievously behind the backs of both his mother and his wife.

SIX

Renee is at school and is absolutely upset. Today, too, Sophie has seized her costumes bag without even giving Renee a chance to explain about her stake in the beauty contest. The situation is totally grim for her since she can't make any sort of excuses at school today, and the school team is leaving for the contest venue in just a few moments. She can see no chance of getting her costumes bag back. She is alone in the class and falls into a depressing state as every minute that elapses only increases her worry.

As Renee sits in sad contemplation, her instructor enters in the classroom looking for her. Upon seeing her student, she says, 'Hey . . . what are you doing here? Aren't you getting ready to come with us?'

Renee is altogether distracted. 'I am sorry,' she says softly. 'I can't proceed further!'

Her instructor is astounded. 'What are you saying?'

Renee begins to sob mournfully. 'I'm saying . . .' she begins, 'I'm saying that I am not going to participate . . . I am not well.'

'What?' shouts her instructor, somewhat aghast. 'What the hell are you saying at this last minute? What will I say to the members of the school management about your withdrawal and our failure in selecting a suitable participant? Are you crazy?' But then the instructor changes her tone as she sees Renee's stress and wonders if her problems can be overcome. She lays her hand on Renee's forehead to see if the girl has a fever.

This compassionate touch stirs Renee's sentimentality, and she breaks into sobbing again. 'Yes, I am disturbed. I have lost my costumes. My bag has been seized by my shrewd sister-in-law. My family is not concerned about my upbringing, affairs, and progress. My daddy is least concerned about my life, and has focused on improving his relationship with our new family member. My mummy would like to see unexpected changes in me, and I am not important to my brother now.' She stops and blows her nose. 'And the whole home is handled by my new sister-in-law,' she continues. 'She does not approve of a liberal life for me and pointlessly interferes in my matters and life without even trying to become my friend first. I want to choose my goals! I can't tackle my sister-in-law over this problem, and it's rather hard for me to go my own way!'

Renee reaches out to her instructor seeking sympathy, and the lady clasps her in a tender hug. The lady is embarrassed no doubt, but she is ambivalent whether to perform her school duty or to believe Renee and tackle this crisis in Renee's young life. She can see that Renee's parents are ignorant of her tribulations and are not providing her any support in her ambitions. She certainly has sympathy for Renee and wants to console her, but at the same time, she wants to overcome the hardship she will endure when the beauty pageant falls apart in the final hours due to the lack of Renee's participation. Just as she feels there is no answer to this problem, she looks up to see a familiar saviour standing in the doorway. She nudges Renee, who also turns to face the doorway.

Matt looks very serious as the two look at him, but he smiles as he says, 'Excuse me! I have heard something is going wrong here. Perhaps a beauty contest is taking place?'

How absolutely reconciliatory his words are to Renee! She rubs the tears from her eyes, but her pout is not so easily discarded.

Matt enters the room carrying an extremely large bag. 'It's quite heavy,' he says to the two. 'I think it is filled with a large number of things that are very important to one particular lady. Can I put it down here?' As he places the bag on the floor, Matt's speech becomes playful. 'I saw a useless bag at my home—I mean, of course, useless in terms of my wife and me. When I examined the contents, I found it could only belong to a participant in a beauty contest. I realized that my old mummy would never participate in such an event!'

The instructor finally relaxes with a big smile. Renee would like to mend her tempers, but she tries to remain angry. Suddenly, however, she finds it too difficult and laughs out loud.

Matt continues his story, 'I recalled that I had met a pretty and smart young lady who is to take part in a big beauty event. She is always in extreme need of flamboyance. Perhaps that lady is not Miss Instructor here?' Matt seems to have come to the end of his speech. Renee approaches him, wanting to take him to task, but instead she lands in his affectionate embrace and holds him for a while. She feels mitigated in her brother's embrace.

The instructor moves forward and puts her hand on Renee's shoulder. 'I think you are not so unlucky,' she says. 'You seem to have a big brother who is willing to back your whims and dreams. Let me leave as I have to look for other participants. You come along soon, and do ask your brother to accompany you. I'm sure you would like him to attend the pageant and see your participation.'

Matt gives Renee an extra-tight squeeze before disengaging her. 'For you, I have taken leave from work today,' he tells her.

Renee tries to be grouchy. 'I do not think I am so important in your account now!'

'All right,' says Matt, laughing, 'then pay me the $250 I have forfeited by not working today!'

'I didn't ask you to be so lavish in order to attend an ostentatious show that's less important to you now than your wife is!' says Renee, continuing to be peevish, yet speaking straightforwardly.

Matt seems taken aback by this taunt, but speaks to save his image. 'You simply cannot blame my wife for your crisis. You should have taken the time to explain your problem to your sister-in-law. You should have told her how important this event is for you. She just wants you to be good in your studies too.' He gives her another quick hug. 'You know that Mummy, Daddy, and I are always there to support you if you tell us how important something is for you, no matter what. And look, I haven't bought a ticket for my wife today! I am going to the pageant only with you. So who do you think is important to me now?'

'I am not a baby that you can sway with your words,' responds Renee, tweaking her big brother's nose. 'I could have taught your lady a good lesson, but respected her seniority and our new relationship since she is new in our family. You know very well how eloquent I can be when I want to prove my point!'

Suddenly Renee looks at her watch and reacts overdramatically. 'Oh my God! We must leave immediately for our destination! It is late!' She points to her bag on the floor. 'And please carry this bag too! You have the honour to be in the company with the future Miss New York Teen, you know!'

'My car is not to be used for carrying such trash!' teases Matt.

SEVEN

At Javits Convention Center, Eleventh Avenue, Manhattan, a good number of participants—approximately fifty—have converged to compete for the crown of Miss New York Teen. The event will last all day, beginning with competition in PT (physical training) exercise, swimming, psychological testing, group discussion, debate, dance, ramp-walk, kitchen work, and fashion parade. It will end with stage interviews of the shortlisted participants.

Renee is there in time to compete as the light physical exercises start at nine o'clock in which participants' health, fitness, stamina, flexibility, and rhythm are tested. Half an hour later, this competition is followed by swimming where bodyline, slenderness, and confidence are tested. In addition, there is a short interaction with the panellists who interview the girls about their leisure interests and ask them if they have had any adventurous experiences that have significantly impacted their lives.

After the half-hour swimming competition, Renee is relaxed and confident that she has lived up to her standard performance to her own satisfaction. After a ten-minutes recess, she is ready to appear in psychology test, group discussion, and debate. She wears a navy-blue blazer and pants over traditional black leather shoes. Her makeup is fresh and light, and her hairstyle is loose and formal.

Group discussion is a half-hour event during which participants are divided into groups of seven. In separate rooms with two panellists for each batch, different topics are distributed in two categories—one to be chosen by participants and another to be chosen by the panellists. Each topic will be discussed for ten minutes. Renee shines in leading the group in sorting out the topic 'teenagers challenged with depression and suicide'. She speaks twice at good length. In another topic, chosen by the panellists—'carbon credits as a measure to alleviate global warming'—she adequately speaks about objectives, facts, updates on results, long-term consequences, policies, and alternatives.

Again, Renee is lucky enough to sort out her favourite topic 'overcoming world poverty in the twenty-first century' in the debate session, during which each participant is given three minutes to amaze the audience with a factual speech. This session ends in a one-and-a-half-hour time interval, parallel to which is also conducted the psychology test—participants are rounded alternatively in two batches for each event.

By noon, the contest breaks for the Friendship Lunch in honour of the mayor of the city. There is good attendance in the lunch hall; indeed, many respected persons of reputation and celebration are in attendance. The lunch runs for one hour. During the next half hour, the participants prepare for upcoming events.

The afternoon session begins with an hour-long ramp walk show. Renee is confident she will captivate the audience and panellists alike as her apparel comprises a tea-length sparkling-magenta satin gown with three-dimensional floral details, matching footwear, and other accessories. Other participants, too, walk one by one down the ramp with the intent to mesmerize viewers with their exquisite dresses.

Afterwards, an hour-long dance competition starts at three. Participants rock with steps of ballet, salsa, jazz, tango, tap, foxtrot, waltz, rumba, and bop onstage with an exciting variety of music, dance steps, costumes, and rhythm. In her ten-minute time slot, Renee thunders the audience with her dance performance.

A half-hour kitchen workshop is held at half past four in the afternoon for the evening refreshment session. Choices made in a questionnaire filled out earlier by participants determine the equipment they are given. The purpose of the test is to analyse the arranging ingenuity of the participants rather than their cooking skill. Tidiness, mood of the moment, and time factor, skill in preparation, and homely approach are the criteria under scrutiny.

The final round begins at six o'clock. This is the showy costume parade. During this competition, points acquired in all other previous rounds are totalled. Some of the girls will be eliminated, and those remaining will participate in the onstage interviews.

Renee is excited to find herself among the last ten aspirants on the basis of merits in the previous tests. In her costume, she resembles a modern fairytale princess. Her sleeveless, drop-waist, square-neckline ball gown flows in two layers—a breeze of elegant blue organza fabric floats over a floor-length dress of white lace). Ruching and sparkling, beaded appliqués make the dress shine. She wears a matching necklace of crystals and gems and big earrings. Her shiny, black hair is swept up in an elegant updo.

One by one, each contestant is questioned about different issues in life and the world. After her introduction, Renee is asked to name the person with whom she would most like to spend her leisure time—her father, her brother, or her boyfriend. With the sufficient confidence and relaxed mood, she steps to the microphone and speaks, 'I would like choose my brother. Even though he is considerably older than I, he is very experienced about the lives of people of my age. He does not live in the past with outdated life experiences, obtained some twenty or thirty years ago. I can talk to him about today's demands I experience in study, future academic choices, and selecting my life's goals. He gives me relevant and experience-based suggestions that help me to cope with life and the world I experience as a child of my generation. He also enjoys and appreciates the styles of the contemporary era. He is my best friend and someone with whom I eagerly share and with whose help I rectify my young ideas. He protects me from advances from unsuitable men, and the lessons he teaches me about men in general will help me to win my Mr. Perfect in ten years or so.'

The audience is stunned by Renee's speech and gives her a standing ovation; indeed, she deserves such accolade for her broad insight towards life. Renee glows and rewards the audience with a beautiful smile. Then the master of ceremonies asks her to demonstrate some of the martial arts that she has been learning. She first begs excuses. 'I would like to beg your pardon as I am not correctly attired for doing a demonstration. Nevertheless, she is quick to apply some easy moves that topple the man to his knees. He reacts good-naturedly, and her big smile again elicits applause from the audience.

Eventually, when the overall assessment is concluded by the judges, including the mayor of the city and all the guests of honour, the selection of Miss Teen New York is made. When Renee's name is announced, she appears graciously in front of the audience, and, as the glittering crown is placed upon her head, blows kisses to them all, in particularly to her brother.

At home, Mr. Dion takes command over the champagne bottle as Renee and Matt excitedly recount the adventures and success of Renee's competition. Mrs. Dion celebrates by accepting the first glass. Sophie is seen taking care of carpet by rolling . . .

EIGHT

Matt is enjoying the proximity of his charming wife Sophie as they sit closely together on the settee in the main hall. Sharing feelings of conjugal love, Matt cuddles Sophie in a passionate embrace. He is impelled by love so he pulls Sophie in his arms and holds her closely. She responds to his show of affection, and they kiss.

But their private moment of intimacy does not last long since they are disturbed when Renee bounds into the room and says loudly, 'I think there is a room for you people inside.'

Despite the interruption, Matt clings to Sophie, expecting Renee to go off. However, Sophie is hesitant and unable to decide what to do, as she is slightly abashed. At least she is scrupulous enough to wiggle out of Matt's embrace as she is no mood to enjoy amorous affection in front of other family members. Sophie rises and heads for the stairs, indicating to Matt that he should follow her to their room, as both of them are in need of each other. Matt rises to follow, but he is impeded by Renee before he can reach the stairs.

Renee seems to feel no remorse over disturbing the romantic couple. Has she no idea about the subject of romance and what propriety she should maintain so that a loving couple can enhance their feelings? No, she is clueless about her brother's romance with his wife. She is motivated only by her own plans. 'Wait,' she says to Matt, 'could I take only five minutes of your time, please?'

Matt is ambivalent now and unable to avoid Renee's request. Renee gently pulls him up to the settee and disposes him for her purpose. She leaves the room briefly and comes back bearing a tray containing some items that appear to be incongruent to Matt. He looks up to see Sophie standing at the bottom of the stairs, watching to discover Renee's motivation.

Renee explains her purpose. 'Dear brother,' she begins, 'I read that people in India celebrate the Festival of Rakhee, which signifies the relationship between a sister and her brother. Usually, a sister ties a scared thread, known as *rakhee*, around her brother's right wrist and prays for his long life, fortune, and protection against any hardship. So, take out your right hand please.'

Sophie advances to the settee and takes a seat beside Matt to watch the proceedings as Renee ignores her and ties a coloured thread around Matt's wrist.

Renee continues her explanation. 'There are varieties of colourful rakhees available on the Internet, but I have failed to procure one for you, as I couldn't assure one would be delivered by today, which is the actual day of this year's festival according to the Hindu calendar, Vikaram Samvat. One my Internet friends from India has actually told me about this festival. She suggested I can work with any sort of thread. The most important part of the ceremony is that I must be jubilant and sincere when I tie my rakhee to my brother. You see?' she finishes. 'One needs only a will to initiate a job!'

Next Renee removes a covered plate from the tray, and uncovers it revealing a pretty assortment of sweetmeats, cakes, and cookies. She picks up a small sweetmeat and puts it directly into her brother's mouth.

'Sisters offer their brothers a treat to express their wishes for their brothers to be prosperous and successful forever. So I think you should finish the whole plate right now.'

Renee pauses for a moment while Matt finishes the sweet. 'And . . . and . . .' she begins as she snuggles closer to Matt on the settee in a jovial but somewhat sneaky fashion, 'And brothers—especially those who earn a lot of money —render gifts to their sisters for the sake of contentment and happiness in the festival, and in particular if they want to continue love from their sisters. So, the next time I will pray for you only when you provide a good gift. This time, I exempt you in goodwill for the sake of the festival!'

Renee surreptitiously moves her hand behind Matt to his back trouser pocket. She is surprised that she does not find his wallet. She is also surprised when Sophie reaches out and grabs Renee's stealthy hand. Sophie has already taken Matt's wallet into her possession. Renee has no other choice but to smile sweetly in order to cover up her failure in appropriating Matt's wallet. She stands up, looks playfully into Matt's eyes, and asks with a little impudence, 'Where is your wallet?'

Sophie intervenes and hands Matt's wallet to him, slapping it crossly in his hand. Matt beams over his wife's cleverness.

Sophie turns to Renee. 'The festival is a good idea to earn—I mean seek—other's money, stealthily!' she says in a taunting tone.

'You can't understand,' says Renee peevishly. 'You don't even have a brother!' She turns her attention to her brother. 'Brother, could you give me fifty dollars? I am leaving soon for a picnic.'

Sophie speaks sternly to her husband. 'That is not required of you,' she says to both Renee and Matt. 'Renee, come to your room with me. And, Matt, I would like you to come as well.'

Once Sophie has dragged brother and sister to Renee's room, she explodes. 'Matt, see all of these wild posters of obscene love!' She tears down a few of them and lets them land on the floor.

'What are you doing?' says Renee in wild protest.

Sophie ignores the young girl and continues to address her husband. 'Take notice of all these grown-up magazines and novels. Look how many there are!' As she speaks, she grabs up several magazines and books and hands them to Matt, who just seems ashamed and unwilling to accept them. 'These spicy music CDs, these boisterous sound amplifiers, these cigarette packets! These are all materials for morbid practices!'

Renee has stopped protesting and appears to be ashamed. But Sophie is unrelenting. 'Have you seen her wardrobe? Only provocative dresses for discos and late-night jazz parties!' She slides the door of the wardrobe open to a brilliant display of fanciful clothing. Matt quickly shuts the wardrobe door.

Sophie is determined to debunk Renee's ruse. 'Today she is planning to attend a picnic at the shore. Take a look in her bag—you are in for a surprise.'

With so many faults on Renee's side, Matt finds himself siding with Sophie. He has no mercy for Renee at the moment and can see no reason to stand by her. 'I am sorry,' he says inexorably to Renee, 'I can't do anything!'

NINE

Renee is practicing her karate kicks while Sheila and Angelina are enjoying fries at the summertime amusement park at Wollman Rink in the Manhattan Central Park area. Angelina purposely speaks to Sheila. 'Renee seems disturbed today!'

Sheila answers in the same tone, 'Yeah! Brother Matt has dared to try to curb all the bad habits of the babe.'

Both girls know that Renee can hear their every word. Angelina feigns surprise. 'Brother Matt? That controlled man?'

Sheila pours on the drama. 'Yeah, he is now totally under his wife's control. He is no longer the obedient puppet of our Renee.'

Renee's kicks become faster and stronger as she listens to the taunts of her friends.

'Are you talking about Mrs. Sophie Dion?' says Angelina, continuing the game. 'Now I can understand Brother Matt's dedication and audacity in controlling Renee!'

Sheila adds fuel to the fire. 'Yup, it's so! Do you know that Mrs. Sophie's cruelty is increasing day by day?'

Suddenly, Renee pounces on the table and sweeps their packets of fries to the ground. The girls squeal in mock fear! 'Do *not* provoke my flame!' she yells at them.

But Sheila relentlessly goads her friend. 'What will you do now? Are you going to allow your sister-in-law to totally rein you?'

Renee glares in determination. 'Never!' she shouts. 'In time *I* will have control over *her!*'

Angelina begins to whine 'But what about our picnic today?'

'Look,' says Renee, mischievously pointing to a passerby. 'That podgy man has more money than he needs. Let me make *smart* use of his money!'

'Whoa, Renee!' warns Angelina.

'But you will land in big trouble!' pleads Sheila.

But Renee has paid them no mind. She has left them and is walking towards the man. As she intercepts him, she purposely rams into him. 'Oh, sorry, macho-man,' she says in mock courtesy. 'Did I hurt you? You seem strong enough to tolerate a light blow from a sweet, young girl.' She tickles his cheek, then turns and waves her hand as she begins to walk back to her friends. The man stares Renee and moves on. Renee comes back to Sheila and Angelina bursting with excitement. She pulls a wallet from beneath her pullover and shows it to them. 'Hi, dears . . . I have managed the money for the picnic! Let's move!'

But a deep voice from behind their backs speaks to them quite formally. 'No, all of you will "move" with me to our department downtown!' It is a very large police officer, and the girls are now worried about this new circumstance.

Renee tries to act innocently to overcome her panic. 'Why? What is the problem we have caused?'

The officer seizes the wallet from Renee's possession. He checks the contents to verify the identity the owner. 'None of you resembles even slightly this photograph of a man. I gather none of you is Mr. William Hutch?' He looks at each of the girls. 'Can any of you tell me how much money is in this wallet?'

Renee is dumbfounded but still quite shrewd. 'Yeah, it belongs to one of my kin . . . and . . . and . . . the amount is around a hundred dollars . . . no, it may be one hundred thirty dollars? I can't tell you the amount as I didn't check when he gave it to me—'

The officer cuts Renee's speech. 'All of you are coming downtown now. We will call your parents to come identify you.'

Sheila and Angelina begin to cry and protest. 'No, we are innocent! Listen to us!' says Sheila.

'We had nothing to do with this money . . . please . . . We are sorry!' pleads Angelina.

But the officer is not listening to either of them.

TEN

As soon as she receives the call from the police department, Sophie rushes to the precinct. She talks with a police lieutenant there. She speaks to the man meekly and humbly. 'I thank you for directly calling our home once you found out these girls' identities. You don't know how much we would have been dishonoured if the story of Renee's brainless, ridiculous act had been published. She is somewhat of a celebrity now, as she has become Miss Teen New York, and would have been haunted by media for a long time and denounced for behaviour that belied the words she spoke at the pageant. I am really grateful for the discretion you showed in favour of Assistant Chief Dion. Thank you for not booking these girls with a charge. As you know, Renee's daddy is a senior authority in the police force, and I fear he might have faced severe degradation over this childish act on the part of his daughter. Also, this case, once publicized, might have impaired my grace too. I am a columnist of good fame, and I might have found it difficult to save face over this.'

As Sophie speaks with the lieutenant, another officer produces the young girls out of their cell. As they enter the room, Sophie gives them all—and particularly Renee—an unnaturally vehement glance.

Renee murmurs to her two friends, 'Oh, God, whom you have sent here . . . my archenemy!'

Sophie turns once more to the officer. 'I again thank you!' she says sincerely. 'And I'm sure that Mr. Dion will also express his gratitude to you.'

'I am forgiving them just on your request, ma'am,' said the officer. 'You know we take our duties and obligations with all sincerity. You should have better control over the minor members of your family, and should have full knowledge of their activities. They are youngsters and prone to show waywardness, but they will create problems for society and for themselves too. I expect that you will be teaching them good lessons. That is why I am giving them a second chance this time—and also giving your family a second chance.'

'I am really sorry for these girls,' Sophie replies with all humility. 'My family—and particularly I—will uphold your admonishment of them and will pay attention to their progress regularly. Please let me get them back into our custody.'

Sophie, keeping a hidden plan, surprises everyone then by approaching the officer's desk and touching a heavy, wooden ruler that is lying there. 'You have a nice baton for executing your service,' she says.

Sophie remains unpredictable. She takes up the ruler and moves with purpose towards the girls. To Renee, her sister-in-law seems unusually aggressive. For that reason, Sophie is able to approach the girl and rip her pullover off her without any protest. The girls are frightened and squeal, and before the officer is able to apprehend Sophie, she strikes Renee's shoulders repeatedly with the heavy ruler until it breaks. 'You bitch!' she shrieks violently at Renee. 'Die for my sake!'

ELEVEN

At home, Renee sits with Mrs. Dion on the sofa. She is enfolded in her mother's embrace, and is sobbing. She is miserably unhappy and does not know how to repent. Other family members stand around them. Matt's subtle smile seems to show feelings of guilt. Sophie's demeanour is quite serious, and she maintains a distance from her husband Matt. Mr. Dion takes out a cigar from his case and inhales rather thoughtfully. He seems rather annoyed in many ways about the current circumstance. He looks gravely at all members of his family and points to the bruises that are evident on Renee's back. 'My child is beaten black and blue today!' He turns to address his daughter-in-law. 'You have punished her appropriately?'

Sophie, in bewilderment, changes her position in the room. She does not know quite where Mr. Dion is going with his words. He continues to address Sophie, and appears to be defending Renee. 'You have my permission to teach my young daughter lessons. I know you care for her and want to see positive changes in her. But do you not understand that sometimes people may learn from their own mistakes?'

This speech takes Sophie aback as it is clear condemnation of her treatment of Renee in the police unit. Sophie catches unmistakably that Mr. Dion is not at all supportive of her method. However, she inclines to debunk Mr. Dion first for his irresponsibility towards his progeny. In a low voice, she says, 'Yes, she enjoys a relationship with me, and I would like to be a good guardian if she is not instructed properly by others.' As she speaks, she intentionally looks straight at Matt, hoping he sees his father's erroneous view of what has been happening and how his family's views are biased against her actions.

Matt feels obliged to agree with both his wife and his family. 'We can deal affectionately with our girl,' he says quietly. 'She definitely looks for our love and attention and for help in sorting out her problems.' Matt wants to solve this issue without a great deal of drama. He feels it unnecessary to chide Renee further and restrict her growth over her minor capricious conduct. He cannot condemn Renee for behaviour that teens sometimes exhibit when they are not properly guided. He understands that Renee is maturing and will learn from her mistakes and be better behaved in future.

But Sophie is irked over unwanted objection to her methods. 'You are absolutely prejudiced, man!' she says to her husband. 'If you were a really sincere brother, you would support a stern approach to the monitoring of the growth of this young girl!'

'I am a good friend to her,' counters Matt. 'You can ask her! We have shared most of the moments of our lives over the last sixteen years, and have enjoyed a loving relationship!'

Sophie is obviously totally offended. 'Don't tell me this!' she shrieks. 'You will know how perilous your "loving relationship" is when your sister is caught in a serious crisis someday because of her absurd practices!' Sophie is stressed over the fact that her sternness in dealing with Renee's upbringing is unappreciated. She is cross that the family members would like to stand by Renee and uphold her liveliness. They do not perceive the situation as serious at all. Frustrated, she decides to leave the room. She pauses at the bottom of the stairs and addresses her husband sarcastically, 'And do enjoy that "loving relationship',' she chirps before turning and bounding up the stairs.

Matt looks at his father. He is a little angry at Mr. Dion for provoking Sophie with his cheeky reaction. He sneers slightly in a witty manner over the embarrassment brought to his daddy—first in his profession because of Renee and second in his family because of his interaction with Sophie. Mr. Dion remains restrained in joining Matt in the smile, which indicates the helplessness he feels. However, his eyes focus on his wife and take on a fresh glitter as he anticipates support from her.

Mrs. Dion desires to mitigate her husband's anxiety. 'I think Renee should harmonize with her new caretaker,' she says, stroking Renee's hair softly. Despite everyone's discomfort, she has suggested a working plan. She looks at Renee before she continues. Then she says, 'All of us should admire our new family member who is only concerned for us and who cares for us.

Matt surprises everyone by loudly supporting his mother's idea. 'I second you!' he shouts, rather more loudly than he planned.

Of course, her brother's response stirs Renee and she moves away from her mother. Giving a solemn look to all members there, she expeditiously moves up the stairs and runs into her sister-in-law's room. She clasps Sophie in an apologetic manner. 'I'm sorry,' she says, obviously seeking a compassionate touch from her senior family member. 'I know I've hurt you.'

Matt dutifully follows his sister into the room. Under the circumstances, Sophie feels obliged to be lenient towards Renee. She speaks coolly, but emphatically to Renee. 'All right, you cool down now! Crying is not the solution to any problem. Instead, you should boldly confess your guilt and show repentance. It's good that you are learning new philosophies and winning laurels in your life. We admire you for your sincerity towards life and your love for us. But at the same time, your bad conduct will put you in peril and cause your family hard times. I know you understand this very well.' Sophie hugs Renee and then stands back. 'You know the stature your family has attained,' she continued, substantiating her ideas. 'And you, too, have achieved some notoriety of your own. What reputation will your behaviour bring to your people? What impressions will you be giving to members of your generation, who may look up to you? And have you ever thought about what it might be like to face the media? They look only for scandalous conduct from celebrated people like you. They will only increase your distress. And all of this together will only cut your chances for a successful and bright career.'

Renee and Matt both know that Sophie has brought up many points that cannot be argued against. Sophie hopes that he has seen her side even though he is used to sticking up for his blood relation. Matt realizes that it i impossible for people to grow up without taking erroneous steps, but he claps quietly to show he reinforces the valuable views his wife has just outlined.

Renee privately decides to keep harmony with her new caretaker, and is relieved to be able to speak up. She grasps Sophie in a firm hug and says between strangled sobs, 'I love you.'

Matt relaxes with a deep breath to see a positive settlement between the two ladies of his home. He gives a thankful smile to Sophie who, of course, is happy to receive appreciation from her husband. Sophie helps Renee to the bed and bids her to lie down. She leaves the room and returns with some healing balm and an ice bag. She loosens Renee's shirt and works to heal Renee's injuries.

Sophie speaks to Renee ruefully and in a motherly way, all the while looking at her husband for his passionate attention. 'Do you know . . . I am . . .' she begins with obviously difficulty. 'I'm surely disgusted by my sister Ashley. She also does not welcome my stern watch over her young life. But whenever I look at her cute countenance, I know I can't allow her to meet any pitfall at this young age. Perhaps I have restricted her life, and that is why she rejects my interference. But, I love her . . .' Sophie sits up straight and wipes a tear from her cheek. 'Today I had conversation with Ashley. She was reserved in an unnatural way.

I would rather see her with a jubilant smile on her beautiful face. Oh, I miss her!'

'Why don't we plan to meet Ashley this weekend?' says Matt passionately, as if he is eager to fulfil Sophie's desire.

TWELVE

In the coming weekend, Renee visits her friend Ashley Jones. They are delighted to be together again. Renee embraces her beautiful friend. 'How are you?' she asks. 'You look enchanting!'

Ashley hugs her friend. 'Thanks! I'm fine. You've won a beauty contest!' she says. 'Congratulations!'

'Thanks!' says Renee, jubilant that her friend is happy for her. 'I have one more reason to celebrate now. I have just received my senior grades—all As! Do you have your grades yet?'

Ashley is clearly still delighted for her friend. 'Congratulation again! I have also passed with all As, and I've been accepted by Cornell University's College of Arts and Sciences for their BA program in economics.' As Renee kisses her friend and hugs her, Ashley asks, 'And what is your plan for higher studies?'

Renee pulls away from her friend, and sits with her hands in lap. 'I am not sure what choice to make,' she admits. 'I've offers from some good undergraduate schools because my brother Matt completed the task of sending applications to colleges. I'm sure he will earnestly suggest the program of study he thinks is best for me. My job was to take tests, write essays, and attend interviews.'

Ashley raises her eyebrows in surprise. 'You ask your brother Matt to make such important decisions for you?'

Renee shrugs. 'No, I don't have to ask. He eagerly manages such matters for me. He insists that I should join programs in aerospace engineering and pursue a PhD too. From his viewpoint, I should choose MIT or Caltech. But, I think I might prefer Cornell University Sibley School of Mechanical and Aerospace Engineering. If I go there, I will be close to my home—and to you.'

As they visit in the sitting room, Ashley's mother Mrs. Jones comes into the room. 'Mum,' says Ashley with great excitement, 'Renee has come to visit us!'

As the older woman extends her greeting, Renee reports, 'Mrs. Jones, I have come to pick up Ashley. Our friends have planned a long drive and a picnic today, and we want Ashley to join us.'

Mrs. Jones immediately looks worried. 'My baby,' she says to her daughter, 'are you really going? Perhaps you should ask your sister for her consent. Let me ring Sophie—'

But Renee interrupts. 'Please stop!' she says, standing and holding up her hand. 'It is enough that I have to get permission from Ashley's sister, who is also going on the picnic with her husband. Please let Ashley make her own decisions so she can to enjoy her life and have some fun.'

With that, the two girls leave the house, climb aboard Renee's motorbike, and zoom off down the road. On the way back to Renee's house, Renee achieves speeds over sixty miles per hour. Ashley is surprised and frightened. 'Slow down!' she squeals into Renee's ear. 'Slow down!'

But Renee listens only to those at home—and listens to them only sometimes. As the motorbike screams down the road, Ashley falls over Renee's back screaming, 'O God! Am I alive now?'

When they reach Renee's house, Renee tells her friend, with no reference to the speedy ride, 'Go inside. I'll be in as soon as I park my bike safely.'

Ashley meets Sophie inside, and greets her sister with a kiss and hug. Sophie is in a happy mood, and is surprised to see her sister. 'You're here! How did you get here?'

'Oh, God, thank you!' Ashley gushes with obvious relief. 'I'm safe! Your Renee is a menace to everyone!'

Sophie looks at Ashley as she tries to figure out what her sister means. Meanwhile, Renee comes into the house, but does not go into the sitting room to join her friend and her sister-in-law when she overhears Ashley telling tales about her. She stands in the hallway, perfectly clad as a tomboy in heavy boots and red leather pants and jacket. Her hair is loose and flowing, and her goggles are perched on top if her head. She carries her helmet under her arm. She listens as Ashley continues her story, 'She is so careless! She rode her bike so fast it made me dizzy! I could have fainted!'

Standing there unnoticed by the other two, Renee sees Sophie's mood become stern and critical. She immediately runs out the front door and around to the back of the house. On the way, she removes her biker outfit and accessories and throws them under a nearby bush. When Sophie and Ashley come out, they find her practicing her stretches as if she had not gone anywhere. Renee flaunts some wonderful kicking steps that she knows will only increase Sophie's bad temper. Sophie comes out with Ashley to take notice of Renee. Seeing Renee in an obviously feigned posture, Sophie holds herself back for the sake of Ashley's visit and the picnic plans. In a huff she announces, 'No one can change and tame this girl! She will remain out of control!'

Soon, they prepare to leave for their long drive. It had been planned that Ashley would ride in the car with Matt and Sophie. But Renee insists that Ashley ride with her on her motorbike even though Ashley begs to ride in the car because she has already experienced Renee's frightening whirlwind speeds. 'Why do you want to hang out with the "old folks"?' Renee admonishes her friend. 'Come with me for a thrilling ride!' Ashley begrudgingly agrees.

Renee, not wearing her helmet, but rather hanging it on the handlebar, kick-starts the bike and rapidly moves into traffic in high gear. This time, she tries to inspire Ashley into enjoying the high speed. Renee asks Ashley to set her favourite music on her iPod, and soon she is driving the bike even faster.

Seeing that the girls are now so far ahead of them, Matt stops the car in a quiet lay-by to see if he can allay Sophie's fears for their respective sisters with his love. Sophie tries to object his flirting, as she is seriously concerned about girls. But Matt insistently pulls Sophie into his arms and pinches her in a naughty mood. It is time for romancing instead of running uselessly behind the girls who are not there to curb their passionate sentiments. Sophie is soon divested of most of her clothes, and Matt is kissing her and fondling her. Sophie eventually succumbs to Matt's love!

Far ahead on the road, Renee and Ashley are being chased by two hooligans on bikes. These boys try to irritate the girls as they crowd Renee's bike and hover around her from all directions. As one of them rides by, he snatches Ashley's iPod and rides away at high speed. Seeing this, and being totally offended, Renee chases the hoodlums, determined to teach them a lesson. She rushes ahead for a tussle with boys, not paying attention to her hazardous speed. Ashley is anxious over the risk. 'Renee!' she shouts in terror. 'Stop! There's no need for a fight!'

But, as the girls approach the boys speeding bikes, Renee's mad driving leads all of them to lose control of their bikes. Renee is thrown onto the road, unconscious. Ashley is not seriously injured, and remains conscious—and whining. The boys are somehow safe because of their meticulous biking skills. They have a chance, so they move to attack the girls. However, Renee wakes up just in time to attack them with well-placed kicks. The guys try to overpower Renee, but she is dexterous in kickboxing and thrashes the ruffians vehemently.

Meanwhile, Ashley has called Matt and Sophie on her mobile phone, and they arrive at top speed to aid in the girls' rescue. At their appearance, the biker thugs leave the scene immediately. Ashley is so dismayed over the miscreants' rudeness and their near disaster that she lands in Sophie's arms for a hug of commiseration.

It takes Sophie only a moment to look around and assess the situation. 'You stupid girl!' she shrieks at Renee. 'Why don't y you apply your head when you are riding? Where do you leave your head?'

Renee stares at Sophie in amazement as Sophie reprimands her and shows sympathy only to Ashley. Matt behaves ignorantly and intuitively finds a chance to gibe Renee; he spontaneously joins Sophie without assessing Sophie's aversion, which is worsening the context and is directly blaming Renee for recklessness and the accident. In his usual outspoken style he comments, 'She has left it (her head) on the bike. Helmet is hanging on the handlebars . . . it seems to be protecting the mirror!'

Renee finds herself alone in an intricate and difficult position. She fights back by turning to her brother. 'You are henpecked!' she shouts.

Everyone is shocked. Sophie is rendered speechless by her sister-in-law's direct and rude denunciation. Matt stands with his mouth agape, unable to say anything.

Sophie grabs Renee by the shoulders. 'Say you're sorry!' she demands, shaking the girl.

'No!' shouts Renee, giving Sophie a cold, dark look.

Sophie continues to shake Renee. 'You *must* say you're sorry!'

'Never!' retorts Renee adamantly.

Frustrated with Renee's objections to her commands, and totally humiliated, Sophie loses control and slaps Renee's face. Renee is aghast. She can feel her cheek turn hot. She cannot stand Sophie's single-minded intolerance. Her response echoes with hotheaded emotion. 'He—is—*henpecked!*' she says.

The grave situation leads Sophie to be obstinately ruthless. She is incensed over Renee's cocky remark and her attitude. Still holding Renee by the shoulders, she gives the girl another shake. 'You have to say you're sorry.' More quietly, she adds, 'I ask it.'

Renee, thus pushed further into a more uncomfortable position responds, 'I still say he is henpecked.' Renee finds she is segregated even further from everyone there. There is no reprieve from Sophie, and Matt, in contrast to his usual behaviour, reservedly does not instinctively protect Renee. Sophie remains determined. In response to Renee's self-satisfied behaviour, she again slaps Renee in protest.

Renee cannot give up now. Breaking into tears, she shrieks, 'He is henpecked . . . henpecked . . . *henpecked!*'

Sophie totally loses control. She continues to shake Renee. However, Sophie's endeavours are suddenly turned against her as a beaten-down Renee resorts to her kickboxing skills in order to save herself and to trash Sophie.

But it seems that Sophie must have taken some lessons in martial arts too, and it becomes impossible for Renee to overcome her 'archrival.'

Matt prefers to remain out of the physical battle. He stands off to the side with an astounded Ashley instead of becoming a scapegoat. Renee is being trounced! It is difficult for her to overcome a potent Sophie. Sophie finally overpowers Renee, who ends up thrown to the ground. She lands near the middle of the road and fails to get up. However, an alert Matt jumps instantly to his sister's rescue. Grabbing her in his arms, he carries her to the side of the road, barely avoiding being crushed beneath the wheels of an oncoming, speeding lorry.

Everyone is stunned and shocked as they watch the lorry pass by without hurting them. Matt holds Renee and rubs her back to show sympathy as she shivers with trepidation. Renee recovers after some time but she is fully enraged. 'No!' she says, pulling away from Matt. 'Leave me! I will teach her a lesson!'

Matt takes a firm clutch over Renee to prevent further physical antagonism, as he understands that Renee cannot defeat Sophie. Nevertheless, in the scuffle, Renee hits Matt with a punch in his belly.

'Okay,' he says. 'Cool down now. That's enough for her.'

Renee cools down and curbs her rage when she realizes that it is only causing her brother to suffer. Matt temporarily relaxes when Renee's anger appears to be assuaged, and Sophie seems to understand the severity of her own misdeeds. He moves with Renee towards Sophie so the ladies can reconcile. He finds he has little to say to his wife. As Sophie joins them, she realizes the perils she could have caused and the severity of the hostility she has flaunted. Regretting her prejudicial conceit, Sophie puts her arm around Renee's shoulder. 'Sorry!' she says.

Matt cannot resist adding, 'I am *not* henpecked!'

THIRTEEN

It is getting late and it is time to leave the scene of the accident. Renee wants to remain clasped in Matt's hug. She is in no mood to jeopardize her relaxed state and face additional trouble when Matt is distant from her. Matt is obliged, in the circumstances, to obey Renee. But he has not yet decided how to solve the newest problem: Sophie does not know how to ride a motorbike properly, and Ashley cannot ride one at all. He knows Renee doesn't want to remove herself from his display of compassion. And he wants to evade going with Renee on the bike. Finally, he decides to send the three ladies along in the car, and he will follow alone on the bike. He decides this despite the fact that there is a risk that the recent hostility between Sophie and Renee may not let them settle graciously. Nevertheless, Matt believes that Sophie will display maturity and won't brawl with Renee any more, in consideration for her youth. But Renee is still not comfortable with Sophie. She is afraid that she might not be able to resist flouting something that would irritate Sophie irrevocably. So Renee rejects the idea and prudently refuses to take a seat in the car. 'Brother,' she demands. 'Get on the bike, please.'

'Oh, *no!*' pleads Matt.

'Oh *yes!*' counters Renee persuasively.

Sophie intervenes and graciously provides clearance for Matt to ride the bike. 'Matt,' she says sweetly, 'you can go on the bike. I will ride with Ashley in the car.' She gets into the car and turns on the ignition. Ashley takes a seat beside Sophie.

Matt is now grumpy. 'You have to ride the bike!' he tells his sister. But Renee moves with determination. She takes off Matt's shirt. Soon, they are on the bike with Renee behind her brother, tied to him with his shirt. Renee leans against Matt and closes her eyes to sham an intention of going for a snooze. Matt rides on to soothe Renee. Nevertheless, he doesn't want to be a tamed person either.

Matt tries to attract Renee's attention by shouting back at her. 'Sophie is senior to you. She is our family member. You should give her due respect and pay attention to her instructions. She will definitely love you as she does her own sister Ashley. And you should be a close friend to her. You will learn a lot from her experience and her devotion to home and family life.' When Renee doesn't respond, he shouts, 'Are you listening? You are growing up and must soon face the challenges of life!'

However, Renee seems lost in her vacuous snorts over Matt's lecture. He recalls the past times when he similarly chided a much younger Renee for enjoying biking at high speed. As they approach the town, several old acquaintances wave to Matt—a member of the traffic police and a passer-by. They remind him of bygone days of his youth.

When they reach home, it is late in the evening. Renee seems lost in sleep . . . like the deep sleep of the very young. Eventually, Matt has to call Mrs. Dion outside to take care of her young baby with great fondness. He calls to her in a childlike voice, 'Mum . . . Mum!'

Mrs. Dion arrives and is delighted to see her children back home. She wants to have Matt comfortable now, so she shakes Renee. She is wise to Renee's pretence, because Renee is now sixteen years old and no longer sleeps like a baby. Notwithstanding, Renee continues with her sham, but there is a big smile on her face as she opened eyes once. There is no other option; Matt has to carry a heavy Renee on his back up the stairs to her room. He rather intentionally and forcefully throws her onto her bed. Renee is now wide awake. As she has received some injuries, she shrieks in protest against the rough handling and again quickly tries to get lost in her bed. Matt is familiar with any number of Renee's dramatic farces. To dissolve this one, he moves to pull Renee's pants slightly down. This leads Renee to immediately come awake. She sits up and holds Matt's hands to put an end to the prank. 'You idiot,' she whispers to her brother, 'don't you have a wife?'

Matt smiles wickedly. 'I thought you were hoping I'd still help you change your clothes.'

Renee snarls over Matt's mischief as he gets up and leaves the room. She leans over the side of the bed and picks up a slipper. But Matt is alert enough to defeat Renee's intention. He flees out the room, and Renee's slipper hits the door he has slammed behind him instead of her intended target.

Later, Renee shares her bed with Ashley. In the next room, Matt lies waiting in the bed for Sophie. When she joins him, she cuddles Matt, enjoying his close embrace, but she is in a rather sentimental state, and wants only to be lost in Matt's love. 'I am sorry!' she whispers. She becomes deeply emotional. 'Renee is like my own sister to me . . . just like Ashley. I shouldn't oppress her. I really regret my behaviour. I'm really sorry!'

Matt feels he must address Sophie's emotion. He strokes her hair passionately as he speaks to her. 'Renee is young and she is different from Ashley, because she has grown in a different atmosphere. Her family is different from your old family, and she expects us to encourage her for her lifestyle and the decisions she makes. I have looked after her for a long time—as a very close friend—and, as you know, I fully support the fact that she should experience every chance and every moment of life. I have developed a positive intimacy with Renee, and she becomes vexed when I stop supporting her, especially when she is upright and correct in her methods. But she has grown naughty and audacious too; nevertheless, she would like to be your friend as much as mine, because she instinctively enjoys intimacy with people and wants to learn many new things from others' experiences.'

In the spirit of goodwill, Sophie quietly pays attention to Matt's words, as she is a mature woman. She kisses him and moves ever closer to him. She is composed and delighted. She tickles Matt's hair and gazes deep into his eyes. Sophie caresses Matt. 'You have been trying to be the friend of everyone here! You have loved Renee since her birth when you were twelve years old, because you wanted to admit new members amiably into your family. After your mother's demise in an accident some two years before Renee's birth, your daddy wanted you to have a positive and intimate relationship with your stepmother so that you would feel loved and cherished properly in your juvenile life. Your father encouraged you to join in the nurturing of baby Renee so that you would develop a stronger bond with Mrs. Dion, who reciprocated by loving you throughout your childhood. More than that—Mrs. Dion arranged our first meeting at a social party of her circle of friends, which included my mother. She has been as pivotal in the strengthening our relationship as she was in the development of it.'

Sophie's reminiscences cause her to experience sombre feelings. 'But I come through a different past,' she continues. 'My father deserted us by divorcing my mother for another woman. There was continual strife between my parents then, because my mother was unable to raise her children alone. Ashley was just a toddler. It was hard times for us, as my mother lacked the proper means and we were challenged for living. At only age twelve, I was not able to help my mother. It was about that time that Mrs. Dion began her acquaintance with my mother. When she came to know our suffering, she helped us in many ways and wanted you to take care of me too. Mrs. Dion introduced you to me, and you soon became my best friend. You protected me from mishaps, and supported me to what I am today. Even when you attended the graduate program at faraway Penn State University, you didn't desert me. I owe you, dear!'

Sophie is lost in emotions as she recalls days gone by. But at the same time, she is earnestly seeking the compassion from Matt that he used to supply without question. Matt smiles and assures Sophie that all is well, and, through their love, they will always enjoy a strong attachment. He sees a new side of his wife, and realizes her dedication to sticking with him forever. He clutches Sophie tightly, caresses her hair, and makes a move for an endorsing kiss.

Unfortunately, however, only troubles can be expected from a naughty Renee, even when she should be asleep. She turns on her waywardness to caress Ashley rather intentionally. Renee ignores all measures of decorum and rowdily cuddles Ashley. Ashley screeches instinctively when Renee teases her while Renee displays an insolent smile even in feigned sleep. But, the disturbance comes to Matt's attention. At first, he thinks it is Sophie's objection to his inflamed love. 'You screamed?' he asks his wife.

Sophie also shakes her head for 'nay' in response to Matt's dramatic reaction.

'Damn it!' mutters Matt as he disengages himself from Sophie's hug. He hurriedly moves into Renee's room where he finds an astonished Ashley gazing at Renee who appears to be lost in sleep despite her prankish smile. 'Ashley,' says a boggled Matt, 'go share the bed with Sophie. Even a ghost couldn't settle in to share this bed!' After Ashley leaves the room, Matt goes downstairs to sleep in the on the settee in the sitting room.

FOURTEEN

When Mr. Dion, in his jogging suit, enters the sitting room with the newspaper, he finds Matt sleeping on the settee. Scowling and twisting his son's ears, he shouts, 'Is this the place and time to sleep? Go out for a jog!'

Matt gets up with a low squeal, but he is not angry as he leaves the room. Left alone, Mr. Dion reclines there, placing the newspaper on the table. Mr. Dion: 'Now I can enjoy a little nap in here!' he says to himself.

After a while, Renee comes into the sitting room. She approaches the sofa from behind and, without looking, pounces on the reclining figure, who emits a loud squawk in response. She jumps up. 'Who is this plump man?' she asks just as she recognizes her whining father. 'Daddy . . . you? Where is Matt?'

Mr. Dion is obviously peeved. 'He has just gone out to find something he can use as a weapon!' he threatens.

Renee gives her innocent daddy a weak smile and recedes away from her daddy. But she walks without turning so she hits Sophie coming into the room with the tea from the opposite direction. Both of them become uncomfortable, however, Sophie is walking carefully so she won't spill the over-loaded tea tray. Mrs. Dion follows Sophie into the room. Renee sulks, because she believes that Sophie is going to be harsh and take her to task again. 'Sorry!' she says softly to Sophie.

Sophie carefully places the tray on the table and beckons to Renee. 'Come here!'

But Renee only recalls the bad experience of the previous day and fears Sophie's revenge. However, Sophie walks up to Renee and takes her into a rather compassionate, sisterly embrace. Giggling with commiseration, Sophie whispers, 'I love you!' She plants a long kiss on Renee's cheek.

Renee is surprised by this unexpected show of affection, and she is in no mood to accept Sophie's love. She pulls back, trying to elude the kiss. 'Oh!' she says, her stress obvious to everyone present.

'Renee,' Sophie says modestly, 'you are going to be an aunt! I am expecting. I am really going to need you!'

Renee grasps her head over the revelation, then hugs Sophie in congratulations. Meanwhile, Ashley comes down the stairs and hugs her sister from behind, having heard the news. Sophie rubs Ashley's cheeks in reciprocal affection.

Just then, Matt rushes into the living room, obviously excited and befuddled. 'Hey Renee . . . Daddy . . . Mummy!' he shouts, 'I am going to be a mummy!' He raps his head at his obvious mistake. 'Oh, no . . . I mean Sophie is going to be a daddy!' As everyone dissolves in laughter, Matt is finally able to get out a correct sentence: 'Damn it!' he shouts. 'Both of us are going to be parents! Yay!'

After a while, Sophie sits before Mrs. and Mr. Dion and speaks to them solemnly. Meanwhile, Matt, Ashley, and Renee have left the room and returned with balloons and a child's trumpet.

As the young people romp with their toys, Sophie addresses her in-laws, 'I rang my mom this morning as soon as I got the news and told her she is going to be a grandmother. She is very happy and wishes to see me. She says she dreams of being a loving and responsible granny to my new baby. I wish to visit my mummy now and share this moment with her.'

Matt hovers over his wife, blowing his toy trumpet to encourage his parents to accede to Sophie's wishes.

FIFTEEN

Matt is reclining on the chaise longue in Mrs. Jones' living room browsing through columns authored by Sophie in many periodicals. His wife is elsewhere in the house visiting with her mother. He is rather lost in his endeavour and his comfortable position. Ashley comes into the room and finds Matt unaware of her presence. As a prank, she sneaks up behind him and pokes a thin piece of paper into his ear. Matt reacts instantly, turning to see who the culprit is, but Ashley has hidden around the corner out of his sight. Matt sulks and looks around as he scratches his ear. As soon as he is comfortable in an alternate position, Ashley again sneaks up behind him and pokes his ear. She immediately runs out of his reach, of course laughing over his awkwardness and helplessness. Matt is chagrined at his own foolishness and for allowing Ashley to achieve the advantage over him. He intends to discipline Ashley for her playfulness, but Ashley has gone out of the room. He can still hear her laughing. He uselessly pursues Ashley, but all he sees is her little wave as she disappears around the corner at the bottom of the stairs. Matt knows he has been defeated, and returns to his place on the chaise.

After a while, Ashley returns to find Matt lost once again in the vulnerable pose. She stifles her laughter and enters in the room to harass Matt again with the paper strip. She calmly and surreptitiously creeps up behind a gullible Matt totally prepared to interrupt his leisure. She moves to poke Matt's ear, but this time she fails to run away as Matt shows great agility. He grabs her arm and topples her down onto the floor. Ashley is slightly hurt but stops trying to escape when she realizes she is caught. Instead, she dissolves into a full fit of giggles. But Matt's temper flares at this derision and he decides on revenge.

He snatches the paper strip from Ashley's hand and drags her onto the chaise. Ashley immediately grasps Matt's intention and she puts hands over her ears as she is pinned down. In spite of her previous attitude of superiority, she begins to shriek and wiggle. This provokes Matt in his attack. He tears Ashley's hands away from her ears and holds onto them as he sits over her to hold her down.

Ashley is unable to wiggle out of Matt's clutch. She is so overcome, she cannot even jeer at her brother-in-law. She tries to convince him to let her go, but Matt is not inclined to listen her pleas. Rather, he mercilessly tickles Ashley's ears with the paper strip. Ashley is laughing so hard and struggling so hard, she thinks she may vomit! Matt is relentless in his attack, so Ashley screams. 'Sister . . . sister! Sophie . . . help!'

Ashley is breathing hard. Through her laughter, she continues screeching for help. Suddenly, Sophie bursts into the room. Misconstruing the scene, she is aghast to see such cruelty being done to Ashley. Matt has noticed Sophie, so, to show her how much he had suffered just a moment ago from Ashley's relentless teasing, he intensifies his attack on Ashley.

Sophie reacts immediately, vehemently pushing Matt away from Ashley. Laughing so hard she appears to be crying, Ashley is so relieved, she clasps Sophie and hangs on in an effort to control her sick state. As she calms down, in order to set Matt up for the learning of a lesson, she tells her sister, with much exaggeration, what has happened. She even produces some tears as she tells Sophie how extremely sick she is feeling. Sophie protectively holds Ashley in her arms, rubbing her back to encourage slower breathing.

Sophie's attitude is aggressively grim, but Matt still feels ridiculed by Ashley and intends to continue his revenge. Unaware of Sophie's disposition, he moves to continue his attack. Sophie, however, changes his mind and vehemently slaps her husband. 'You rascal!' she shrieks at him. 'How dare you touch my sister?

Are you trying to treat her as you treat Renee, who is always ready to fulfil your morbid desires?'

Of course, Matt immediately notices his wife's quick change of mood, but he refuses to take the blame for the situation, and in retaliation, matches his temperament to that of his wife. He slaps Sophie. 'How dare you blame my sister? I will not allow you malign her in such a way!'

At the harsh touch of Matt's rather big and strong hand, Sophie feels tears trickle out of her eyes and down her cheeks. Distracted by her tears, she pushes Ashley from her embrace and abruptly punches Matt hard in the face. Matt falls back as a result of this sudden strike.

It takes a while for Ashley to realize what is going on, but when she does, she is amazed and tries to make Sophie understand exactly what is going on. 'Sister, stop! Listen to me! It's not what you think!'

But Sophie does not want to hear; rather, she grabs a hefty brass pot from a nearby table and smacks Matt over the head just as he is struggling to recover from her punch. Helpless to break up the fight, Ashley finally runs out for the help before anyone is seriously hurt. She returns with Mrs. Jones in time to see Sophie continuing her attack on a bleeding and nearly-unconscious Matt. 'Oh my God!' says the shocked lady.

SIXTEEN

Renee runs ahead Mrs. and Mr. Dion and approaches Ashley in the hospital waiting room. Mrs. Jones follows her daughter to greet Mrs. and Mr. Dion and console them over Matt's condition. She is obviously aggrieved. 'We are so sorry over Matt's condition. We tried to hold Sophie and Matt apart and keep them from harming each other, but we were too late and my baby had already destroyed him! We saw Matt unconscious and bleeding profusely! Without delay, we brought him here. Right now he is in the operating room. I am worried because he received several rather severe head injuries!' A hush prevails among them as they worry over Matt's dreadful condition.

Finally, Renee asks her friend, 'Ashley, tell me what happened that has resulted in the sorry state of my brother.'

Ashley looks at her mother sheepishly as a request to speak. Receiving a nod from Mrs. Jones, she says, 'Renee, I am really sorry! I didn't know my awkward prank was going to prompt such a deplorable situation. He was totally lost in a magazine when I teased him by tickling his ear with a piece of paper. In retaliation, he took a firm grip over me and tried to tickle me the same way. I screeched for help, and when Sister Sophie arrived she considered the situation much more objectionable than it really was. We never believed she had a temperament that would lead her to slap Matt and accuse him of filthily behaviour. I tried to explain, but she wouldn't listen. He became aggravated, and he slapped his wife! She lost control over herself and hit Matt with a brass pot. I ran for help, but by the time my mother got there, the damage had been done. We . . . we are now hoping for a good recovery for your brother soon.'

Renee is shocked to hear this story! She looks at her sister-in-law, who is sitting alone in the corner of the waiting room looking sadly disturbed. Grieved, Renee moves quietly towards Sophie, but she suddenly loses control. She lunges at Sophie. 'You bloody hag!' she shouts, grabbing the distracted woman.

Mrs. Dion immediately takes hold of Renee, but the girl wiggles out of the older woman's grasp. 'No!' she shouts. 'Leave me! I know what she has done to my brother! I will kill her!' As she speaks, she tries to strike Sophie with one of her kicks.

Renee is almost to hit Sophie, but before this Mr. Dion—watching Renee's behaviour and being alert—took control of Renee. 'Control yourself!' he admonishes, pulling her away from Sophie. 'We are not here to fight!'

Sophie looks blankly at the assembled family members. Finally she speaks in at attempt at explanation. 'You don't know what the scene looked like when I entered the room! I thought Matt was harming Ashley. I couldn't control myself . . . I didn't know what I was doing.'

Just as Sophie finishes speaking, the doctor comes out of the operating room and approaches the family. 'The patient is in need of blood—B positive—and we lack extra units of that type. Does anyone here have B positive?'

Renee jumps up. 'I also have B positive blood! The patient is my brother! I'll do anything I can to help!'

The doctor gives the family a few additional details and then leaves with Renee just as a police officer enters the waiting room. He addresses the assembled family members formally. 'Our department has information that a man has been admitted here with serious injuries he received as the result of an attack. I have to prepare a detailed report!'

Mr. Dion (intervening immediately with his prudence): 'Officer, my son is undergoing surgery right now. Allow us to wait until we hear he is out of danger, and then we will be able to talk to you.'

The police officer makes a note in his notepad. He asks Mr. Dion to comply with some formalities in the investigation of the case. After Mr. Dion assures cooperation, the man in the blue uniform says, 'I expect cooperation from you, sir, in solving this case!'

The police officer leaves after saluting Mr. Dion. The family members are stupefied; Sophie seems in a state of dismay.

SEVENTEEN

The next day, Matt has recovered his sensibilities and is sitting up in his hospital bed surrounded by family members—all except Sophie, who hesitated to come to the hospital for fear she might not be able to cope with seeing the injuries she caused her husband.

As they chat with Matt, the police officer again pays a visit to the family. He is there to record Matt's statement, having discussed some preliminaries with Mr. Dion about Matt's recovery and receiving permission from the doctor. As the officer begins to question Matt, however Renee cannot resist interfering. 'Yeah, my brother Matt's life was threatened by his own wife, Sophie! She is prejudiced against the Dion family—'

But Matt cuts her off. 'Renee!' he yells as sharply as his condition allows. 'Go out for a while!'

Renee quiets down only a little. 'Brother,' she pleads, 'tell the man about the brutality of that unjust woman!'

Matt appears offended and once again addresses his sister. 'I'll say it again: please get out!'

Renee is astounded at her brother's reaction. She can't believe that he may be in favour of exonerating his wife, and she is cross that he had spoken to her so harshly. It's hard for her to overcome her sentimentality, so she turns and runs out of the room in dismay.

Meanwhile, Matt wants to deal with the police officer who seems rather surprised and concerned over Renee's demeanour.

In a reserved tone of voice, he addresses the policeman. 'Officer,' he begins, 'you should not be swayed by what you have previously heard about my injuries. It was simply an accident. I was irritating my sister-in-law with silly pranks. To get me to stop teasing her, she ran behind me and began chasing me. But in my attempt to get downstairs quickly, I stumbled and fell all the way down. I received many serious bruises on my head and was unconscious when I landed at the bottom. It was my wife and in-laws who helped me and got me immediately to hospital. I am indebted to them for their expeditious help!'

The police officer takes a note of the statement made by Matt, but he is not surprised over Matt's stand in the case. It does not take long for the man in uniform to grasp Matt's motivations to hush up the actual events. Indeed, Matt wouldn't like to see Sophie behind the bars; neither does he want his relationship with Sophie to end.

The policeman, in pursuit of his duty, offers Matt a chance to change his statement. 'Are you certain about your statement? Would you like to make any changes? I have heard there is a possibility that there is another side of the story that is being concealed. We are still going on with our investigation, and by the time we are finished, you may wish you had altered your statement.'

But Matt is not deterred by the officer's formal words. 'I do not alter my statement,' he tells the officer. 'I am not feeling well. You must consult my daddy if you would like to proceed in any direction beyond my statement.'

The police officer is reluctant to disturb Matt further. He proceeds to have Matt sign the statement. Mr. Dion speaks with the officer for a while before he leaves.

Mrs. Jones is delighted to see that Matt is inclined to forgive Sophie. She sees Renee enter the room with a very grave attitude, and notices that Matt is not inclined to make up with her just yet. It's Mrs. Jones instead who boosts Renee's spirits. 'Matt,' she says cheerfully to her son-in-law, 'you are very lucky to have a sister like Renee. She has given blood for your recovery!'

This statement softens Matt a bit towards his sister, and he feels somewhat abashed about his recent attitude towards her. He looks at Renee with an expression of gratitude. This stirs a subdued Renee, and she runs to her brother. As she clasps him in her arms, she bursts into tears.

Matt is a bit confused. 'Hey, stupid!' he says. 'I am too sick to be hugged like this!'

Renee is now sobbing openly. 'I hate you!' she blubbers. 'You don't know . . . how much I love you!'

Matt looks into Renee's eyes. 'We all love each other,' he tells her. 'We love Sophie too! You are crying uselessly. She may have hurt me, but we have to tell her how much we love her. We all have to get along together now. Sophie is pregnant, and we are hoping our new baby will bring lots of new love to our family!'

Mrs. Jones comes forward just in time to relieve Matt by taking Renee into her embrace and providing affectionate conciliation.

EIGHTEEN

Later that afternoon, the police officer arrives at the hospital with two junior officers. He politely addresses the members of the Dion and Jones families, who are still visiting with Matt, except for Sophie and Ashley, who have remained at the Jones' home. 'I have come to arrest Mr. Matt Dion.' When family members begin to complain, he continues by way of explanation, 'Mrs. Sophie Dion has pressed charges against Mr. Dion for attempted rape against her sister, Miss Ashley Jones. Mrs. Sophie Dion said that, after the attack, Mr. Dion lost his footing at the top of the stairs when Miss Jones was trying to chase him away, and he received his injuries as he fell to the bottom.'

Every single person in the room is stunned. Matt's own mother, Mrs. Dion, totally perplexed, is the first who is able to speak. 'This is absolutely wrong!' she declares. 'How has she come to such an explanation? We would like to talk with her before you make your arrest!'

'I'm sorry, ma'am,' says the officer, politely addressing the lady, 'but Miss Ashley has corroborated her sister's story and insists that Matt is himself totally responsible for his state.'

The family cannot believe what they are hearing. Mr. Dion approaches the officer. 'Please,' he says. 'You should wait. My boy is injured. You should have the necessary permission from the doctor to move him from the hospital. And, of course, I will pay the necessary bail for his release!'

The police officer agrees to talk to the doctor according to Mr. Dion's directive. 'Bail, however,' he explains, 'will be set by the judge by the court.'

Distraught, Mrs. Jones, wanting an explanation from her daughters of the accusation they have made, returns home immediately. Walking through her front door, she calls desperately, 'Sophie! Ashley! Girls! Where are you?

Soon Ashley comes running into the foyer, but she is in a desperate state and clasps Mr. Jones. 'Mum!' she whispers.

Mrs. Jones is grave. 'What happened? What led you to make this desperate and incorrect statement?' As she speaks, Sophie joins them. She stands rigid and seems emotionless.

Mrs. Jones turns anxiously to her older daughter. 'Sophie, what's this stupidity? He is your husband! Do you want to see him behind bars?'

Sophie turns her frustration against her mother. 'Would you like to see *me* behind bars instead?'

Mr. Jones ridicules Sophie's interpretation of the circumstances. 'What are you saying? Don't you see how much your statement has disturbed all of them? Matt is recovering from such a bad condition, and now you have decided to get him imprisoned? Don't you know that he gave a statement that would acquit you of any wrongdoing?' Exasperated, she turns to her younger daughter. 'And, Ashley . . . you?'

Ashley is obviously still in extreme despair. 'No,' she says quietly but firmly. 'I am sorry for the bad treatment of my brother-in-law, but Sophie made me back up her story! She stressed to me how important it was. I was so nervous when the policeman questioned me, and I totally gave up and told him what Sophie told me to say. You can understand that, can't you?'

'Ashley!' hissed Sophie, pulling roughly at her sister's arm. 'There's no need to prattle on so! Who is that man to you anyway? Listen, you have to cooperate fully with me! You are *not* going to withdraw or change your statement!'

'Why are you so distressed?' says Mrs. Jones, horrified. 'This situation is not hopeless! What impression will you give to your new family who loves you so much? What do you want actually?'

But Sophie is not deterred by her mother's pleas. 'What do I want? A divorce! I have asked my attorney to prepare the necessary papers.'

Mrs. Jones and Ashley stare at Sophie in a stupefied state with their mouths agape. Mrs. Jones wraps her arms around both of her daughters and prepares to weather the tornado.

NINETEEN

Renee visits the Jones' home, desperately looking for Sophie. As she runs up the stairs towards Sophie's room, she calls, 'Sophie! Sister Sophie . . .' When she enters the room, adamant in her desperation, she finds Sophie cold and aloof. 'My dear Sophie,' she entreats, 'what wrong has happened to you? I can't believe you are showing this amount of hostility!'

Sophie remains hateful. 'I don't want to see any of you,' she says bitterly. 'You'd better leave—immediately!' she shouts.

Renee refuses to leave and speaks in anguish. 'Why do you continue this petty animosity towards us? Are we your enemy? Why don't you understand that your actions will destroy our world? My brother Matt is completely aghast to know you want to break up your relationship. He can't bear your prejudicial behaviour.' Renee is close to tears, but carries on nevertheless, trying to rouse Sophie's sympathy. 'You have had a love relationship with Matt for a long time! Both of you loved each other very much. Think of those days when you could hardly bear to see Matt perplexed, and how you would comfort him with tearful sentiments. When he suffered a gap in his life after his mother's demise in his childhood, you gave him solace and sought to give him love that would be a substitute for the love his mother would have given him.'

Sophie is obviously irked by Renee's pleas, but remains contemptuous. 'Oh, you are so cranky. Just shut up!' Sophie knows she is breaking promises she made once. She is unable to find any explanation for her sudden lack of commitment; therefore, irrationally, she approaches Renee and physically pushes her away. 'I say get out of here!'

Though astounded by Sophie's treatment of her, Renee remains determined to achieve her purpose in some way. 'No!' she says, grabbing Sophie and pulling her towards the door. 'I have come to take you back into our family.' But this causes Sophie to be irritated anew. She pulls away from her young sister-in-law and slaps her full on the face. 'Renee!' she shouts. 'You are being foolhardy!'

Renee is shocked and dumbfounded and immediately begins to cry. With obvious hurt showing in her eyes, she looks at Sophie. 'Why do you hate me?' she asks, continuing her persuasive discussion and not taking heed of the tears that are now streaming down her cheeks. 'I want you to come back to our family. Come with me . . . please! I am leaving to join college in this fall semester. I won't be staying at home to disturb you if you find me a cause for breakup with Matt. He loves you more than anything else and can't bear the separation from you, as you know. Both of you can sort this out.'

Renee is now gently pleading since she is determined to defeat Sophie's acrimony and encourage her to withdraw the charges against Matt. Nevertheless, Sophie is standoffish and unwilling to overcome her resentment. She lacks courage to change her mind, and in her narrow-mindedness, determines to hurt Renee. She becomes fanatically intolerant and slaps Renee again; indeed, she even lands some serious punches on Renee's body. Although Renee tries to show restraint because she has come here for peace rather than violence, she cannot help but utter cries over the repeated strikes she is receiving. Mrs. Jones and Ashley suddenly burst into the room. Mrs. Jones instantaneously takes Renee in her arms, sheltering her from Sophie's trouncing. At the same time, Ashley seizes Sophie and tries to pacify her.

Mrs. Jones is aghast. 'Why the hell are you beating this innocent girl?'

Sophie is calm in her hostility. 'Ask her to leave here without delay!'

Renee is unable to do anything but cry over her injuries, both physical and sentimental. 'No! Please come with us,' she pleads with Sophie. 'You must reunite us . . . we all love you!'

TWENTY

Later that afternoon, after Renee has returned home and told her parents about her experience, Mrs. and Mr. Dion have come to the Jones' home to see if they can offer any help. As they sit with Mrs. Jones in the living room, Sophie walks into the room. She is surprised to see her in-laws, and decides to deal with them firmly. Harshly, she says, 'I am very sorry about this matter, Mrs. and Mr. Dion!'

Mrs. Jones is appalled at her daughter's blatancy. 'Sophie, where is your decency?'

Mr. Dion, however, grave in his demeanour, but smiling affectedly, says 'Sorry, Sophie? For what?' His intention is to compel Sophie to confess her culpability in her own words. His expertise in the field of police work has trapped Sophie in a corner.

Sophie is obviously flustered, and struggles to maintain restraint and propriety. 'You know very well!' she hisses.

Mr. Dion maintains his cool demeanour. 'Yes, Sophie, you would definitely like to be sorry for your many behaviours, isn't that right?'

Sophie feels vulnerable and can find no words that are suitable for a retort. Mr. Dion has implicated her neatly.

Mr. Dion continues in calm understanding. 'I think you would like to be sorry for a lot of matters . . . first of all for disregarding our love, which you fail to acknowledge even on a small scale.' Mr. Dion is trying to take advantage of the small amount of humility that Sophie is displaying at the moment, as she surely must feel trapped.

But Sophie is determined and defends herself against his condemnation. 'No!' she yells. 'None of you likes me! If you did, you would not have allowed that police officer to threaten me with the consequences of the law!' She turns to her father-in-law. 'Daddy, at the very beginning, you could easily have restrained that officer from proceeding in the case. But you wanted to see me in jail! And your young daughter, who is always combative towards me, revealed my actions to the police. It was her words that started this whole thing!'

Mr. Dion is amazed at this revelation, but is still determined to conciliate Sophie. 'You are still resentful! You are the one who has so badly complicated this case! I could not interfere with the work of that police officer because he is not under my direct supervision. I would have had to contact a number of subordinate officers to restrain him from performing departmental duty, and I have to be careful not to attract media attention. They would be happy to report that I have been high-handed and have used my position for my own good in the case. I did what I could to encourage the officer to close the case when Matt gave his story in a show of good will and an attempt to save his relationship with you.'

Mrs. Dion, grief-stricken, intervenes. 'It's only your narrow-minded approach to Renee and her behaviour, which lacks both compassion and uprightness, that led her be so agitated that she told the officer of your unjustified callousness towards your husband. Today again, you have attacked her and beat her mercilessly! She is shattered, unable to think, and unable to take her meals—she is utterly repressed.' She becomes more and more angry as she speaks. 'I am appalled by your temper! First it led you to cruelly injure Matt, and despite that, you are now inclined to allow him to suffer responsibility for your own violence. Nobody is ready to believe that you are his wife and that there has ever been a love relationship between the two of you.'

Sophie slyly bluffs her way through her mother-in-law's anger. 'Matt is himself responsible for his condition today. And Ashley has admitted it!'

Mrs. Dion (offended): 'Just shut up! What prompts you to conceal the truth?'

Sophie tries to explain her thoughts. 'I can't tell the truth! It's not easy for me! I am a celebrated columnist and cannot impair my career and interests. I am accountable to my career and fans because I write about commitment and integrity. But Matt can help me here . . . he will solve my problem by agreeing to the divorce.'

Mrs. Dion is clearly agitated and full of ire. 'Sophie, you are a cowardly, despicable woman!'

Rigid and unyielding, Sophie responds, 'I am sorry. I know this hurts all of you, but I see this as the only settlement possible. I will plead to the court to exempt Matt, and Ashley will retract her statement. We will go on as usual with our lives, and Matt will not be required to die for me.'

Everyone is shaken by Sophie's unjust and selfish behaviour and reasoning.

Mr. Dion, whose tolerance has been overcome by bitterness, says, 'Of course nobody will die for you, despite your lasting cruelty. But my son does, in fact, love you, and hopes you feel similar love for him. He will never support your wickedness, and I promise you that he will definitely defeat you in court. You cannot produce good and useful writing when you are lacking in goodness yourself. You are definitely not a good role model for your women readers.'

Sophie remains firm and does not seem interested in any of her family members' concerns or advice. She stands up and walks out of the room without looking back.

TWENTY-ONE

The Supreme Court of New York City assembles. A large number of attendees are generating a goodly amount of gossip as Justice Michelle Fisher is announced and takes her seat. She quiets the crowd and begins to speak, 'The court meets to hear the case of attempted rape on Miss Ashley Jones by Mr. Matt Dion. Mr. Dion is charged by Mrs. Sophie Jones Dion, wife of Mr. Matt Dion and sister of Miss Ashley Jones. Additionally, Mrs. Jones has requested a divorce from Mr. Dion on the basis of the disrespect shown by Mr. Dion, the damage to her feelings and career, as well as incessant harassment of her at Mr. Dion's home by the Dion family. However, Mr. Matt Dion has countered her accusation by claiming that Mrs. Sophie Dion is psychologically disturbed and has misconstrued his interaction with Miss Ashley. He further claims that Mrs. Dion has always been withdrawn and has failed to recognize his love for her. Mr. Dion requests that Mrs. Dion be treated by a psychologist. He is compassionate. He and his family are eager to reconcile with her. He feels there is no relevant reason for the breakup.' She pauses and nods to the prosecutor. 'You may proceed.'

Mr. Thomas, the prosecutor, rises and respectfully addresses Justice Fisher. 'Justice Fisher, as Miss Ashley Jones has attested in writing to the attempted rape against her by Mr. Matt Dion, I consider it meaningless and a waste of time to discuss any further this part of the case. I therefore move directly to advocate for Mrs. Sophie Dion's request for divorce.' The prosecutor turns to address the entire assembly in an effort to dramatize his next remark. 'The reason Mr. Dion is contesting the divorce is purely monetary. Mrs. Sophie Dion earns a handsome income in her writing profession.'

Renee has been listening to the prosecutor and can remain still no longer. Just as he finishes his sentence, she jumps up and shouts, 'No! That is not true! We do not need her money! We do not want it!'

Justice Fisher raps her gavel to quiet the crowd. 'Order . . . order!' she calls sternly. 'You are not allowed to intervene in these proceedings,' she warns. 'Sit down. If you interrupt again, I will have you removed from this court.'

With Renee seated again, and subdued, the prosecutor continues to address the court. 'Mr. Matt Dion is joined by his family members, Mr. and Mrs. Dion, and his sister Renee, in his quest to receive a good part of Mrs. Sophie's income. These family members conceal their monetary desires by professing to love Mrs. Dion, and when she is not inclined to yield to their demands, they harass her by various means and they do not allow her to take part in family activities and matters. They encourage Mr. Matt Dion's young sister, Miss Renee Dion, to repeatedly harass Mrs. Sophie Dion and teach her lessons that force her to remain within the Dion family's clutch.' Again, he sweeps the assembly with a dramatic glare. 'In this regard,' he continues with a serious overtone, 'I would like to call Miss Renee Dion to the stand to testify about her harassment of her sister-in-law!'

Renee walks shakily to the stand and complies with the necessary swearing-in etiquette. Mr. Thomas begins insincerely. 'Miss Renee, you won a beauty contest! You are so gorgeous!'

Renee shows her gullibility as she answers simply with a tentative smile, 'Thanks!'

The prosecutor continues in his insincerity. 'So gorgeous, in fact, that you can manipulate any person and wrap him or her around your little finger!'

Renee smiles but she is being duped. 'Yes . . .'

The prosecutor continues, 'And you can apply pressure and tact in handling such a person if he or she is slightly adverse to your inclination.'

Renee only smiles as she is confused by his words. She does not respond for fear that she will only be supporting the prosecutor's views. He continues, 'So one day recently when you were short of cash, you picked the pocket of a complete stranger. Unfortunately, an alert policeman witnessed that theft and arrested you.'

Renee is stunned. 'Who has told you this?'

Ms. Segal, the defence lawyer and the Dion family are upset over Renee's gullibility. Unfortunately the prosecutor has been able to consistently exploit the proceedings.

The prosecutor ignores Renee and address the judge, 'Justice Fisher, this young girl has had the mercenary intention to harass her sister-in-law. When she was denied money from Mrs. Sophie Dion, she resorted to pick-pocketing, which brought disgrace to Mrs. Sophie Dion's social status. But, Mrs. Sophie Dion took hasty steps to hush up the case, not only to protect herself, but to prevent the punishment of the young girl and disgrace to the high administrative position of Mr. Scott Dion as it reflects on his family.

Renee squeaks desperately, 'It's not true!'

The prosecutor affects a sulk. 'Not true? It isn't true that you hit Mrs. Sophie hard when she visited the hospital to take care of her injured husband? Even when you knew that she was pregnant? Didn't you take advantage of the situation to exploit the moment and teach Mrs. Sophie a lesson?'

Renee was confused. 'I was provoked! And, under the circumstances, I forgot that she was pregnant!'

Mr. Thomas was undeterred. 'All right . . . will you tell me a truth please?' Renee gazes at the prosecutor as he feigns patience and good manners when he speaks again. 'You use your beauty to reign over your brother Mr. Matt Dion, don't you?'

Renee doesn't answer; rather, she fixes the man with an awkward look because she fears further absurd accusations from him. He does not disappoint her. 'Or is it a sham on the part of Mr. Dion?' He deliberately pauses until he sees that Renee is listening. 'Is it a sham on the part of Mr. Dion to gain your confidence and incite you to fulfil his morbid desires?'

Renee can no longer remain calm. 'You bastard!' she shouts, half rising from her chair. The members of the Dion family begin to talk agitatedly among themselves. The defence lawyer moves to intervene, but Renee has more to say. 'He is going beyond proper limits to accuse me in a filthily manner! He is trying to defame us . . .' she cries.

The defence lawyer silences a distraught Renee with a hand signal and addresses the judge. 'Objection!' she says. 'Justice Fisher, I beg your pardon on the behalf of this young girl. This is her first visit to a courtroom, and she is unable to sustain the intractable defamation she is receiving at the hands of the prosecutor. I ask, Justice Fisher, that you kindly direct Mr. Thomas to back off his attack on this young woman's sentiments and grace.'

Justice Fisher nods and turns to Renee. 'Young lady, you should behave yourself! This is a court of law, and you must behave accordingly when you are here.' Then she turns to the defence lawyer. 'Your objection is sustained. But I expect your clients to maintain the dignity of the court; otherwise I will charge *you* with contempt of court!'

With her best manners, Ms. Segal says, 'I promise, Justice Fisher, we will maintain our decorum.'

Ms. Segal whispers to Renee in a conciliatory manner, 'This is a court. You must behave properly! If you don't cooperate with us, we will lose the case. Your clumsiness will allow the prosecutor to prove you guilty, and Matt will be sentenced to a prison term!' When she is finished, she turns back to the judge. 'Justice Fisher, will you grant me permission to stand with my client so that she will not feel dismayed and will be able to show courage and decorum?'

Justice Fisher smiles over the lawyer's prudence. 'All right, but you are asked to uphold the dignity of the court.' She turns to the spectators. 'We will recess until one o'clock.'

TWENTY-TWO

The prosecutor, Mr. Thomas, obtains permission to speak to the judge. 'Justice Fisher, Matt Dion took advantage of Miss Ashley Jones' innocence and credulous relationship with his family to molest her. It was only the intrepid and courageous interference by Sophie Dion that protected the young and innocent Miss Ashley's safety and virtue!' He continued before she could stop him. "Sophie Dion chased Matt Dion away from Ashley Jones, and as he fled, he tripped and fell down the stairs, damaging his head seriously.' He took another breath and continued. 'The Dion family accuses Sophie Dion of causing these same injuries by hitting Matt Dion over the head with a heavy brass pot. Their statement is nothing more than a scam to get Sophie Dion sentenced for attempted murder. How can anyone expect Sophie Dion to remain married to a husband who has attempted to rape her sister?'

The judge starts to turn her attention to Ms. Segal the defence lawyer, but the prosecutor has just a few more words for her. 'Justice Fisher, I praise Sophie Dion for having the courage to prosecute her husband for his flagrancy, and I am proud to represent her. I ask that you consider the case in light of Mrs. Sophie Dion's future needs. I think the evidence is clear now for an expeditious hearing.' Just when everyone thought he had said all he had to say, he spoke again, turning to Ms. Segal. 'Ah, perhaps, her attorney would like to say something in her defence!'

Ms. Segal addresses the court respectfully. 'Justice Fisher, it seems that the prosecutor is in a hurry to conclude the case without listening my clients' side of the story. Indeed, he is not even allowing his own client to be cleared of the accusation that has been imposed in the counter suit.'

Ms. Segal returns to sit with the Dion family, careful to display a relaxed demeanour to show that the prosecutor's antics have not caused permanent tension. She leans over to Renee and speaks to her quietly. 'Relax, my dear. The prosecutor has imposed a lot of accusations against you and your family. I know you would like to refute all of them. But considering your youth and your inexperience with the court proceedings, I would like to ask you to be calm as you tell the court your story. Address your thoughts one by one. I and the court are here to help you if you have a problem in meeting the court's expectations!'

With that, Renee is asked to take the stand once more. The defence lawyer looks at Justice Fisher for permission to begin questioning. When she receives it, she begins calmly. 'So, Miss Renee Dion, first please tell us about your involvement in the pick-pocketing incident, which has been presented here as an act on your part engineered to harass Sophie Dion!'

Renee looks awkward and seems unable to speak. Ms. Segal waits patiently for her to gather herself. Finally, looking at her family members for courage, she begins. 'I was in a festive mood on that day when I was out with my friends. I wanted to prove to them how smart and daring I was. I admit that I wilfully stole that man's wallet. The police officer, when he learned of my background, considered it an unwise youthful prank, and therefore let me go with an admonishment because the man did not press charges after he got his wallet back. But my sister-in-law Sophie would not listen to me or anyone else. She was so angry at what I had done that she thrashed me brutally with a big wooden ruler.'

Ms. Segal, with a light smile, asks a question on a completely different subject. 'And would you like to tell us about your rapport with your brother Matt?'

Renee looks down and then speaks with great emotion. 'We have enjoyed a warm affinity for the seventeen years of my life. My brother has taken an interest in my growth since my birth and checks my progress in all areas every day. He doesn't want me to be a fool in the world so he directs me in every aspect of my life. His concerns have led me to succeed in many events—academic, athletic . . . even fun endeavours. My dad and mum have always worked hard and are not always at home, so I consider myself lucky to have a sincere older brother to take care of my upbringing along with my parents. I am grateful that he helps me pick out my clothes and teaches me society's finer disciplines and manners. It's totally another matter that I now have to face the world of people like Sophie and her lawyer who are nasty and jealous of the rapport I share with my brother.'

Renee feels so hurt over having to clarify her stand that she is unable to control herself. She suddenly gives up in the proceedings and runs to her brother. She falls into his arms for conciliation. The court is quiet as people watch the devastated young girl. Matt detaches himself from her embrace, but rubs her hair affectionately to comfort her.

Ms. Segal sees this as a positive point for Justice Fisher's consideration and is in no mood to allow the prosecutor to change the current mood of the court. She politely addresses the judge. 'Justice Fisher, I think we have heard sufficient testimony from Miss Dion for now. I am in no mood to harass a young girl who has been traumatized. But, I would like to call Mr. Matt Dion to the stand to clarify his statement and his view of Mrs. Sophie Dion.'

TWENTY-THREE

Ms. Segal, the defence lawyer, is not happy with the way the prosecutor is handling the case. She continues her case by giving Matt the chance to share his views. 'Mr. Dion,' she says to her client, still on the stand, 'I think you are also as hurt as your young sister is by the accusations imposed by the prosecutor. You may take this opportunity to explain your sentiments and clarify the facts as you see them.'

Matt seems detached as he speaks. 'Yes, I am hurt by what the prosecutor has said, but also by the accusations of my wife Sophie. I don't know how she can be so angry with my innocent actions with her sister after she herself has committed so many violent acts, which have only hurt all of us. Indeed, her accusations are utterly mind boggling and only reflect her sick mind. I would definitely like to join my sister Renee in denying all of her accusations!'

Matt seems encouraged by his own testimony. 'I don't know how Sophie can think I could ever harm my own girls Renee and Ashley, especially with carnal desires! Sophie and I have shared many cordial and mutually loving moments . . . private in nature. I don't know how she can think so nastily of me . . . of what I might do to innocent girls. The accusation of attempted rape made by my sister-in-law Ashley Jones is totally wrong, and I would like my mother-in-law to come forth herself and tell the truth as she has witnessed the event and my innocence. It depends totally on them to tell the truth and prove my innocence. Only they can help me in my attempt to save my connubial life with Sophie.'

Mr. Thomas, the prosecutor, sees a chance to refute Matt's testimony. 'Objection, Justice Fisher! Matt Dion is playing with the sentiments of his wife's family in an attempt to make them think about his marital relationship with Mrs. Sophie Dion. But this has no basis now with regard to his offence. He should rather confess or refute the accusation in a direct way!'

Ms. Segal has an answer. 'Justice Fisher, Mr. Dion has total freedom to relate his sentiments and his information, as this is a family tribunal.' Justice Fisher sustains the defence lawyer's argument.

Matt, detachedly continuous in his testimony, this time directly addresses the judge. 'Justice Fisher, it is totally incorrect that I have married Sophie just for an interest in her earnings. I invite you to ask her to recall any occasion when anyone in my family asked her for money for any reason. We have never done so. My dad holds a high administrative position in law enforcement. My mum earns handsomely through her medical practice. My own employment as an aircraft engineer allows me a very comfortable life without having to ask my parents for money. I don't know how Sophie has come to conclude that we are after her money. Yes, she earns good money, but we don't need it! She only imagines this because of her prejudiced temperament. We have been good friends since we were at school. When we were growing up, she sometimes got into trouble with our friends for her antagonistic behaviour, but I helped her overcome many of these altercations* and helped her maintain her friendships. Later, when we fell in love, we solved many of our misunderstandings just by sitting together and talking things through. I think this time too we ought to sit together just for a moment, talk about what has happened, and try our best settle things in goodwill. Life is filled with ups and downs . . . and we are about to become parents!' Matt speaks calmly and with great sentiment. 'Justice Fisher, please give us an opportunity to meet and resolve our problems before you grant this divorce. That's all I have to say.'

As Justice Fishers makes a few notes about Matt's statement, members of the audience begin to breach the quiet by breaking into conversation. She raps the gavel to remind everyone to keep quiet and respect the dignity of the court. She looks at the defence lawyer to proceed further.

TWENTY-FOUR

The defence lawyer formally addresses the judge. 'Justice Fisher, I would like to call Mrs. Sophie Dion to tell the truth!' Sophie takes the stand and performs the necessary formalities. Ms. Segal skilfully addresses her. 'Relax, Mrs. Sophie Dion! Nobody is going to hurt you; certainly not in the detrimental manner with which you destroyed your husband Mr. Matt Dion' head!'

Even though Sophie has thoroughly prepared herself for her testimony, she loses control directly. 'He was himself responsible for his bad condition! He hurt my family and me in all respects!'

Ms. Segal is undeterred. 'Yes! Your family members really are hurt by these proceedings, and I mean by the accusations you have imposed on them by trying to obscure the truth from the court.'

Sophie makes a move to protest with a heated argument, but she recalls her careful preparation, and instead just gives the defence lawyer a stunned look.

Ms. Segal continues. 'This is not a healthy practice when your family is trying hard to overlook your attacks and your false accusations as easily and as soon as possible! You are a celebrated person. You have a responsibility to your work and your readers. Oh, sorry,' she says, interrupting herself melodramatically. 'Your husband suggests that you are psychologically ill and perhaps unable to take justified steps in making things right and owning up to the truth.'

Sophie's stance becomes rigid as she feels the lawyer is turning up with excessive temerity so Sophie fixes the defence lawyer with a look to browbeat her. Ms. Segal smiles affectedly at the judge. 'Justice Fisher, Mrs. Sophie Dion seems to lack the ability or willingness to be cooperative with the court. Her prejudices may interrupt the proceeding. I beg you to excuse her, as I believe it is her mental condition that is causing her behaviour.'

Justice Fisher only smiles instead of taking notes in order to show her good will for both sides. Sophie seems to struggle over her brush with the defence lawyer.

Ms. Segal continues. 'Well, Mrs. Dion, I do hope you do not wish to be seen as psychologically ill. Instead, I think you should try your best to let go of your prejudices and admit the truth, which is the innocence of the Dion family!'

Sophie takes control of herself, remembers her preparation, and calmly responds, 'What are you saying? What sort of prejudices have you seen in me? It is totally beyond my perceptibility. Both the court's time as well as my own time is precious, so if you would like to prove some facts by interrogating me, you had better come out with direct questions relevant to the case and easy to answer!'

The defence lawyer, however, is not easily deterred. 'Mrs. Dion, the court is asked to recognize your psychological state in deciding this matter. To perceive you better, the court would like to know about your views regarding your life and your family. In this regard, kindly tell us about the rapport you share with the Dion family!'

Sophie speaks confidently. 'Well, Matt has recounted the truth about our friendship.'

Ms. Segal immediately addresses the judge. 'Justice Fisher, kindly note that Mrs. Dion sanctions Mr. Dion's statement!'

Justice Fisher feels obliged to make a note despite the consternation of Sophie. Ms. Segal encourages her to proceed, but her speech is cautious. 'We have enjoyed a lot of gracious moments and tried to understand each other as best we could. But I failed to discover his latent violent tendencies. Indeed, we enjoyed a successful connubial life. I never realized that he would violently seek sexual appeasement from women in his own family, as he did with my sister . . . and in his own home . . .'

Ms. Segal interrupts her. 'Well, you cannot understand this man even though you have been close to him, but you have come to accept that he desires younger women? Doesn't this tell about your prejudiced approach in your perception of your husband and your intention to malign him and ruin his relationship with his family members?' Then Ms. Segal immediately changes the subject. 'And what's about your rapport with other members of the Dion family?'

Sophie becomes rather reserved in her demeanour. 'I always tried to have good relationship with my new family. But, they have failed to appreciate my dedication and love and have never allowed me feel like an integral member of the family.'

Ms. Segal speaks affectedly 'So, will you substantiate your statement by telling us about some incidents that describe the deportment of family members?'

Sophie seems rather confused. 'There have been many incidences every day that demonstrate the excessive nature of the members of the Dion family. Renee was motivated to harass me often, and Mrs. and Mr. Dion continued to overlook her mischief. These were common occurrences against me, an outsider. I don't know where to start.'

The defence lawyer raises her voice to attract the court's attention. 'Have you forgotten that Mrs. and Mr. Dion are your mum and dad? You have hurt them through your actions. You hurt them even in your old home when they visited you with good will to forgive you without question and bring you again back into the family. They were still affectionate to you because they recognize and understand their son's love for you, and his need for you. But you demanded a divorce without considering the hurt to their sentiments . . . and it was only for the sake of your social status! You said you would appeal to acquit Mr. Matt Dion of the accusation you made against him, but you do this only because you hope it will boost your image as a lenient woman after you have proved yourself a strong woman by destroying him!'

Sophie squawks her objection. 'No! That is wrong!'

But Ms. Segal does not heed her interruption. 'Oh, no? But do you say it wrong that Mrs. and Mr. Dion both work long hours and they do not have time to think about or observe the intricacies of the relationships among their children. And, when they relax, they would like to have intimacy and harmony among family members?' Do you not think they would like a happy ending to this whole affair?'

When Sophie does not answer any of these questions, the defence lawyer continues in her robust manner. 'Can you also deny that you have often thrashed and beaten Miss Renee whenever she did something you considered improper, even though she sought your compassionate proximity and affable love? I say that your violent dealings with your sister-in-law have been sick! Many times your actions have proved hazardous to her life! Why, she barely escaped being crushed under a lorry when you threw her to the ground in anger. Why do you take such a violent and harmful approach?'

Sophie opens her mouth as if to speak, but Ms. Segal turns to address the judge. 'Justice Fisher, the accusations made by Mrs. Dion are only baseless products of her own imagination, brought on by her prejudicial constitution. It is easy to see, from a psychological and a sociological viewpoint that Mrs. Dion is psychologically ill, and I think nobody can deny it!'

Ms. Segal turns to Sophie. 'Mrs. Dion, we have given you a chance to admit the truth, but you have insisted on concealing it from the court. But I will tell the truth. You can go now and wait in a relaxed mood and accept what happens next!'

TWENTY-FIVE

After Justice Fisher has performed some requisite formalities in the proceeding, the defence lawyer continues her interrogation by calling Ashley to the stand. As Ashley is sworn in, a hush prevails in the court as attendees prepare to listen to crucial evidence in the case.

Ms. Segal, considering Ashley's testimony to be most pivotal in the case, begins her questioning. 'Miss Jones, are you comfortable here? Are you dismayed by the dignity of the court? I think you may feel more comfortable than your peer who, in the earlier part of these proceedings, lost control over herself due to lack of experience. Or you may feel similar awkwardness. I will try my best to overcome any dread you may feel!'

Ashley sits without any emotion and appears to be comfortable with the requirements of decorum as demanded by the defence lawyer. Ms. Segal moves towards the real heart of the case. 'Miss Jones, we encourage our young people to participate fully in solving our problem here, as we consider them our citizens of the future. They are important for tomorrow! Therefore, I ask you to be honest and take your responsibilities towards your family seriously.'

The prosecutor jumps to his feet. 'Objection, Justice Fisher! The defence is trying to pressure my client to consider relationships and her responsibility for continuing . . . I mean . . . encouraging Miss Jones to consider the sacrifice that is necessary for continuing a relationship. The defence can't use such motivation to oblige my client to sacrifice by considering unnecessary responsibilities!'

Ms. Segal turns to the prosecutor and addresses him seriously. 'Mr. Thomas, you shouldn't consider Miss Jones as your client. She is independent and bound by the court to tell the truth! We are considering her as a witness. She must tell the truth even if it jeopardizes her relationship with her sister and other members of her family.

Ms. Segal, having a nod from the judge in approval of her continuing, goes on with her questions. 'Miss Jones, you have been represented to this court as a victim of attempted rape. However, you know better what actually happened. Did Mr. Dion actually attempt to violate the innocence of your youth? Your truthful answer will alter the outcome the proceeding of the case. Kindly speak the genuine truth to the court and help us to unravel the crucial mystery in the case!'

As Ashley glances all around to assess the mood of her family members, she perceives the gravity of the court. 'I am very sorry that the situation has become so complicated that we must proceed in this way.'

Ashley's words catch the attention of the court, and they wait eagerly to hear her divulge the truth. Ashley tries her best to be detached and undeterred. 'I can't understand what we are going to achieve by destroying each other and by bringing disgrace to ourselves. Similarly, I didn't understand that my awkward mischief would result in this petty confrontation. My sister Sophie misinterpreted the result of the playful prank I played on my brother-in-law. Her interpretation resulted in a serious physical fight between her and her husband. I tried to tell my sister that her accusations were not true and that she had better stopped fighting. I couldn't convince her, so I ran out to call my mother. But by the time we returned to take control of my sister and brother-in-law, we found Matt unconscious in a bloody state. We immediately rushed him to the hospital for medical care. What really happened to me has not been truly presented in the court. I seriously condemn my sister's behaviour and temperament in dealing with her husband, and I again seriously deny the accusation that Matt made any attempt to attack my modesty!'

Ms. Segal visibly relaxes. 'Justice Fisher,' she says, 'I think Miss Ashley's statement corroborates the statements of my client and represents what truly happened. Therefore, I consider it useless to dispute further, and I recommend concluding the hearing here.' She turns to the prosecutor. 'Of course, Mr. Thomas may proceed if he is inclined to continue the case!'

The prosecutor, admitting the defeat, addresses the judge. 'Justice Fisher, I request the court to drop the assault charges against my client. I also request, Justice Fisher, that the court considers the reserved state of Mrs. Sophie Dion's mind in the context of the statement of Miss Jones. That's all, Justice Fisher!'

Justice Fisher makes a few notes and addresses the court. 'The court is adjourned.'

Renee runs to Ashley and clasps her tightly as she emits a rapturous squeal of exultation at the outcome of the proceedings.

TWENTY-SIX

At home, Sophie chastises Ashley for her lack of integrity and intelligence in handling herself in court. Ashley tries to embrace Sophie as she speaks. 'Sophie, why are you disturbed? Nothing bad has happened, and we are very glad that all of us are going to settle down and leave our differences behind us!'

Sophie pushes Ashley away in anger. 'Leave me! Who are you to me? Go to live with the man and develop a rapport with his family! You would put me on gallows! But they will be not happy when you try to be part of their family!'

Meanwhile, in the town, Matt waits at a street corner near the shops, leaning over his car. To his surprise, he is suddenly surrounded by a group of seven men. They soon make their intention clear to him. One of them steps up to Matt and grabs him by the shoulder. 'Do you know,' he snarls to the others, 'This man is very prudent not to repudiate his wife, a smart lady with smart money. We will teach him that a celebrated woman like her needs a better man than this futile specimen!' With that, he and the other men begin to assail Matt with various tools and weapons. His life is seriously in danger!

But the attack is interrupted when Renee enters the scene. Though Matt is putting up a good fight with these goons, she knows he cannot defeat all of them, especially as his injuries have not healed. She walks into the fracas and addresses Matt. 'Brother, you should not be fighting when you have just overcome such serious head injuries. You should have told these men about yourself! Or you should have told them I was coming to help you.' She points to a clear spot next to his car. 'Just stand there for a moment.' Then she amazes everyone present. She storms the goons with her superior kickboxing prowess. Soon she has toppled every one of them, and they lie injured on the ground.

TWENTY-SEVEN

The court again assembles to give the verdict.

Ms. Segal, the defence lawyer, speaks to the judge. 'Justice Fisher, as we have reached this point in the case, I recommend that Mrs. Sophie Dion should go for psychological treatment. Recently, I have procured a diary belonging to Mrs. Dion in which she writes about her mental condition; indeed, she has written that she would seek death if she faced defeat in the court over the matter because she wouldn't be able to endure having thus to face the world and her fans. Justice Fisher, I think that is sufficient to prove that Mrs. Dion is challenged by a confused state of mind. I request, Justice Fisher, that you sum up the case in favour of my clients.' She hands the diary to the judge.

Sophie looks grudgingly at Ashley as she considers Ashley responsible for her defeat in all respects. Meanwhile, Matt gets up and seeks permission from the court to make a statement. The judge invites him to take the stand.

Matt is grave and perplexed. 'Justice Fisher, I beg your pardon as I decide to abide by my wife Sophie's demand for divorce. I cannot bear that she would prefer to leave this world than remain with me. I only hope that she might someday have renewed feelings for me and return to me once she attains good sense of mind. I do love her.'

Justice Fisher speaks when Matt is finished. 'The court finds that the prosecutor's accusations are totally baseless and motivated only by the plaintiff's compromised state of mind. At the same time, the court finds Mr. Matt Dion at fault for not observing that his wife needs treatment; indeed, I recommend that they both should seek psychological counselling. The court sees no reason that Mr. Matt Dion and Mrs. Sophie Jones Dion should be granted a divorce, especially when both seem psychologically disturbed and when there is chance that they can work together for an amiable settlement in their own good interests. The court encourages the couple to get counselling and work together to solve their differences as suggested by the defence attorney. This court is adjourned!'

After a while, Sophie intercepts Matt on the outdoor steps of the courthouse. Matt is astonished at the outcome of the court case, and Sophie is earnest over the verdict. She feels a determination within herself. Matt would like to stare into Sophie's eyes to understand the determination he sees in her. Sophie is the first to speak. She speaks surely, but with some reservation. 'Perhaps you would again like to sit with me for some time. If you do, maybe you will be able to see my problems.'

Matt feels confident, now, that they may be able to solve their disagreements, and he offers her an endorsing smile. 'I think I would like to have that opportunity. In fact, I would like to always have that opportunity.'

Sophie looks sad and speaks softly. 'I think you won't have that opportunity. You have won the case. I feel you will always be intolerant of me and you will persist in defeating me as time goes on. You have defeated me with your love. But I ask your permission to say one thing in favour of settlement. May I?

Matt looks into Sophie's eyes with an expression of consent; he is eager to hear Sophie's words.

Sophie looks straight into his eyes and speaks in a clear voice: 'I love you!' She moves into his arms and settle's in his embrace. Matt seals the deal with a kiss!

Renee and Ashley have been watching from the entrance to the courthouse. When they see their siblings embrace, they run down the steps and clasp Sophie and Matt in a big family hug. From a short distance, Mrs. and Mr. Dion and Mrs. Jones watch their children in happy settlement. With the glitter of tears in their eyes, they wave at the reconciling group. With this behind them, and a new baby in their future, the entire family experiences a new bond of love.

Cast of Characters

• **Renee**

Renee is one lead character of *Henpecked* who is not just pivotal in one part of the story but by whom this part of the story survives—she is the most 'live' part of this family drama before the story shifts focus instinctively towards the Matt/ Sophie relationship. If the merits of the character of Renee are not recognized, or if the part is not played and directed with due attention, *Henpecked* may fail to achieve its worth. Renee is prominently leading in the first part of the screenplay while her protagonist image is admired enthusiastically by her family. This is because she is, in a sense, smart, elegant, intelligent, bold, boisterous (maybe too much so), childish (and bubbly), lovable, affectionate, gentle, attentive, and sensitive. Besides, she is also presented as a bit sexy. In this light, she must be beautiful, a feature that becomes conspicuous and necessary in many scenes—(i) during the marriage celebration she hovers to deliberately enslave with her endearing pulchritude; (ii) throughout the teen beauty pageant, she is fascinated by her style; (iii) after being vindicated and beaten by Sophie at the police station, and also when healed by Sophie later at home, Renee's torso is undraped, revealing her dazzling structure; (iv) in the fight with Sophie during the long drive, Renee dazzles with her prettiness; (v) finally, when she thrashes the mercenary ruffians, her structure is emphasized. Her comeliness is bewitching, whether she is wearing her school uniform or fancy outfits during beauty contest. She must remain beautiful throughout the rest of the story as well.

Moreover, the complex character Renee is highlighted throughout the story, to the point that we suspect positive 'sentiments' that are not delineated by the story itself. Whether she is chided by Matt during interrogation by police officer or beaten mercilessly by Sophie in a prejudiced manner or accused in the dirtiest way by the prosecutor in the court, Renee displays that she is emotional as well as sensitive. Needless to say, Renee displays her sensitivity as she pays attention to her family. She decorates her brother's room on the eve of his marriage; she ties a Rakhee-band to Matt and prays for his well-being in order to strengthen her bond with her brother; she donates blood for his recuperation; she fights the hooligans who attack an injured Matt. And she does everything in an upbeat mood and with great enthusiasm. Overall, Renee is in the pink—pretty, jolly, frolicking, and rocking. Renee's personality beats as the heart of *Henpecked*.

What I may foresee in Renee is a role model!

- **Ashley**

We learn who this character is and how important she is in the second part of the story. She is, above all, beautiful—and beautiful as only a sixteen-year-old can be. She appears as the young, charming, and lovable babe of a family. However, she is looked after, and therefore leads a restrained life. Moreover, this causes her to be innocent and vulnerable. Whether seeking relief in Sophie's arms after the accident met by Renee during the long drive or stating truth in the court, or exhorting Sophie for her reunion with Matt, Ashley retains her innocence and integrity and upholds their significance in life. Therefore, she embraces the truth instead of supporting the prejudices of her sister. Besides, she is absolutely feminine; therefore, she observes the people around her, and learns how to tease her brother-in-law. Most important, her innocence, cuteness, and integrity are her best assets, and she sufficiently exhibits this boldness in each moment of her part in the story.

- **Mrs. and Mr. Dion**

These are upbeat parents. Nevertheless, they do not interfere unnecessarily in their children's matters since they are firmly assured of the 'goodness' rooted in their son and daughter. But they are ready to tackle their children's problems and they do come forward with guidance when necessary. They also do not like to hurt or discourage any member of their family. Rather, they participate in fun experiences with the youngsters. However, they are soft and sensitive too. When Matt is injured and disturbed in his marital life, they are most concerned and advise Sophie to reunite the family. They are clearly hurt when their son is struck with misfortune. Similar is their approach towards Renee's growth. They insist that she follow the pathway of right and truth. When Sophie is let down by Matt who intentionally defends Renee from Sophie's stern lessons after the pickpocketing incident, Mrs. and Mr. Dion wisely advise Renee to be remorseful for her culpability and harmonize earnestly with the new custodian in the family. After all, they are good parents, are experienced, and look only for positive interests and happiness of the family.

- **Sophie**

Sophie is the heroine of this story—a superwoman who has qualities to lead, at least to lead her man and his family. She is adroit in all tasks, possesses perspectives for a good life, and strictly commands her world with practicality. As society demands today, Sophie is a woman with enough confidence, prowess, and aggression to maintain a hold over her world that includes her new family too, and although she is not upheld to rein with her prejudices and faces opposition, especially from another young woman—Renee—Sophie's integral characteristics of reasonability and competency help her as she seeks to be a superwoman in today's society. Needless to say, there are obvious 'clashes' between two the superwomen as the relationship between them forces them to clash often. However, being the female lead of both the story and the family too, Sophie is much superior to Renee and therefore dominates, even prejudicially, since she feels she must be responsible and central to construct her world into the society she wants and endorses. She insistently abides by a strong feeling that she is right and she must lead her world with her perceptions.

On the other hand, Sophie is feminine also as she sincerely desires to look after her family's affairs. In this aspect, Sophie precisely and ebulliently takes care of home chores and respects the senior members of her new family. At the same time, she is yielding to her husband whenever her husband wants a close relationship with her. Instead of being just an 'angry woman', she has the welfare of the family in mind whether she gets Renee acquitted at the police station, or thrashes Renee in a fight during the long drive for defending Matt's esteem, or guards Ashley from Matt's clutch, or browbeats the defence lawyer in the court. Also, Sophie feels strongly, as every woman does, that her husband ought to reinforce her views, lifestyles, and advances in her husband's family. Therefore, Sophie broadly wants to be part of each activity of her family where she seems to pursue a hidden aim to rein.

After all, Sophie is also beautiful and does not mind using her looks and her charms to enslave her man. She maintains a tall, svelte, and chiselled bodyline so as to appease the romantic approaches of her man. Her looks as well as her acquiescence always enhance the romantic mood of her husband. Furthermore, Sophie appears to be competing with two young beauties. Therefore, Sophie thrashes Renee in a fight without even being hit. She tries to spurn the defence lawyer when the defence thwarts Sophie in the court. In all these scenes, Sophie's beauty is evident, whether she is compliant or she is fretting and fuming. This way, she is a fascinating element in the story—not ready to be conquered ever.

- **Matt**

The lead character emphatically is not just the hero of the story. He above all takes on the foremost place—he is amply cool throughout, pleasing to every person of his world, innocent although mischievous, tolerant, affectionate, and live hearted. Above all, he leads when others fail. He doesn't seek dominance; rather, he leads by supporting and standing by in time. He wants others to lead and lets others take responsibilities. He also knows well his responsibilities; therefore, he evenly supports his wife and sister. In each scene, he is there to correct whenever correction is required, and he tries to keep everyone happy. Besides, he is jolly and jaunty as well as prankish and fun loving.

Moreover, Matt is not just practical in worldly affairs. He interacts with others with a personal touch and healthy motivation. He sustains and respects his sister-in-law's pranks and joviality and becomes childish in his amiable enjoyment of her sentiments. His attitude is to introduce 'delight' in encounters with his acquaintances. Because of this attribute, he is never inclines a bit to desert Sophie even in their bitter battle. Rather, he is adequately calm and prudent as he rejects the prejudices of his wife and wins her back. And his interests lie in moving together with all people of his world instead of disappointing anyone with a wrong step. His conscience and discernment are good enough to thrill people, keep harmony, and follow realistic ways too. And his ability to discriminate sometimes is not one sided, but rather aims towards a good settlement for everyone involved.

Matt is a 'soft-target' and is under the control of every other character. He would like to enjoy playing out this feature of his life. Matt has traits that make him the sort of man everyone wants in his or her family. A woman couldn't ask for a nicer, cooler, or more handsome man than Matt. His parents anticipate their adult children to be cool, cheery, and devoted to their family and siblings. As they grow, they should be supportive, encouraging, and compassionate in their progress. It may be greatly desired in any family that, after marriage, members should actively join together with good spirit rather than seek a separate world. Furthermore, people also long for successful marriages that last forever in the interests, happiness, and unity of family.

However, in today's complex world and with today's hectic lifestyles, most guys wouldn't want to be a guy like Matt. Specifically, no man wants to be considered 'henpecked', even in the most remote way! The character Matt may not appeal very much to guys, but I know every woman will want her own version of this character to cherish forever! Matt is an upbeat guy, absolutely positive in his disposition and sincere in his efforts to overcome bad moments, misunderstandings, and bad outcomes. Matt is not just a good guy; rather, he lives up to the expectations of the people he loves. And with all these attributes, Matt is seen as a jubilant guy in his world. We are happy that the character Matt wins his desire at the end of the story, and this gives the story its worth.

About the Author

I am swayed mostly by a self-professed duty to pick a wide variety of subject matter to write about. I compose passages about life, people, and settings and all the action that develops when they interact. I am quite sensitive too to current lifestyles and the emotions of my characters. I hope this is reflected in my writing. But anyway my intention is not to hurt you!